The world's preeminent
photojournalists
and thinkers depict
essential issues
of our time

WHATMATTERS

Created by
DAVID ELLIOT COHEN

STERLING

New York / London
www.sterlingpublishing.com

STERLING and the distinctive Sterling logo are registered trademarks of Sterling Publishing Co., Inc.

Library of Congress Cataloging-in-Publication Data

What matters : the world's preeminent photojournalists and thinkers depict essential issues of our time / [edited by] David Elliot Cohen.

    p. cm.

  Includes index.

  ISBN 978-1-4027-5834-8

  1. Social history--21st century--Pictorial works. 2. Social problems--Pictorial works. I. Cohen, David, 1955-

  HN18.3.W53 2008

  909.83'1--dc22   2008011116

10 9 8 7 6 5 4 3 2 1

Published by Sterling Publishing Co., Inc.
387 Park Avenue South, New York, NY 10016
© 2008 by Western Arts Management, Tiburon CA USA

Distributed in Canada by Sterling Publishing
c/o Canadian Manda Group
165 Dufferin Street
Toronto, Ontario, Canada M6K 3H6

Distributed in the United Kingdom by
GMC Distribution Services,
Castle Place, 166 High Street, Lewes,
East Sussex, England BN7 1XU

Distributed in Australia by Capricorn Link
(Australia) Pty. Ltd.,
P.O. Box 704, Windsor, NSW
2756, Australia

Printed in Singapore by Tien Wah Press
All rights reserved

Sterling ISBN 978-1-4027-5834-8

FOR INFORMATION about custom editions, special sales, premium and corporate purchases, please contact Sterling Special Sales Department at 800-805-5489 or specialsales@sterlingpublishing.com

YOUR COMMENTS WELCOME:
editor.whatmatters@gmail.com

A contribution has been made in support of Green Press Initiative (www.greenpress initiative.org), whose mission is to work with book publishers to conserve natural resources, preserve endangered forests, reduce greenhouse gas emissions, and minimize impacts on indigenous communities.

CREDITS

Photograph, page 1, by Maggie Hallahan

Photographs, pages 11-12, by Eddie Adams and Joe Rosenthal are reproduced with the kind permission of The Associated Press

The archival glacier photographs, pages 26-27, are reproduced with the kind permission of the Minister of Public Works and Government Services, Canada.

Jeffrey Sachs' essay originally appeared in an earlier form in *Time*.

Photographer and author portraits in *What Matters* are © 2008 by their respective photographers and reproduced with their kind permission:

Stephen Voss, page 47, by Charlene Voss Kannankeril

Gerd Ludwig, page 81, by Peter Wintersteller

David Marple, page 81, by Lan Chan-Marples

Omer Bartov, page 97, by Hans Glave

Raymond Depardon, page 97, by Clemence Rene Bazin

Samantha Power, page 113, by Walter Chin

Marcus Bleasdale, page 113, by Karin Beate Nøsterud

J. David Ake, page 139, by Todd Rosenberg

Paul Fusco, page 153, by James Wendell

James Nachtwey, page 173, by James Nachtwey

Lauren Greenfield, page 191, by Robert Leslie

Juliet Schor, page 191, by Gary Gilbert

Stephanie Sinclair, page 221, by Mitchell Prothero

Judith Bruce, page 221, by Douglas Menuez

Ed Kashi, page 241, by Kristin Reimer

Michael Watts, page 241, by Ed Kashi

Sebastião Salgado, page 257 by Giorgia Fiorio/Contact Press Images

Helen Epstein, page 291, by Peter Peter

Maggie Hallahan, page 307, by George Jardin

Brent Stirton is represented by Getty Images.

Marcus Bleasdale, Lauren Greenfield and Stephanie Sinclair are represented by VII Photo.

Sebastião Salgado is represented by Contact Press Images and Amazonas.

Thanks to:

A WHAT MATTERS

Photographs That
Can Change the World

CONFEDERATE
DEAD AT
PETERSBURG.
Photograph by
Mathew Brady,
1865

EVERY MEDIUM HAS ITS OWN MAGIC, and since its invention in the early nineteenth century, the particular power of photography has been its ability to freeze an instant in time and serve it up for deliberation. Pioneering photojournalist Henri Cartier-Bresson (1908–2004) famously said that great photographs capture "the decisive moment." When used in the service of social and political advocacy, a series of these decisive moments—a photo-essay—can catalyze real-world reforms.

Photography is older than audio, video or interactive media, but it captures decisive moments better than any of them. Since the mid- to late nineteenth century, photojournalists have created photo-essays that have exposed unpleasant truths, advanced the public discourse and championed social causes.

For real photojournalists, using photography this way is a basic instinct and an essential element in their code of conduct. In the 1860s, Mathew Brady trundled his wooden camera and tripod out to Civil War battlefields to make albumen silver prints that belied

by DAVID ELLIOT COHEN

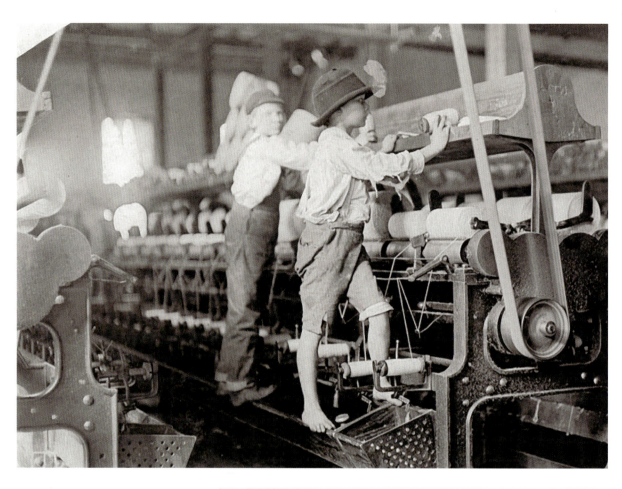

BIBB MILL NO. 1.
Photograph by Lewis Hine,
Macon, Georgia, 1909

FIVE-CENT LODGING.
Photograph by Jacob Riis,
New York, 1889

the glory of war. Three decades later, Dutch immigrant Jacob Riis used camera and flash powder to expose brutal conditions in New York's tenements, and from 1908 to 1912 Lewis Hine, an investigative photographer for the National Child Labor Committee, crisscrossed America photographing children as young as three working twelve-hour factory shifts.

These photojournalistic "muckrakers" (Teddy Roosevelt's coinage) actually got results: Riis' tenement tableaux, initially published in *Scribner's Magazine*, convinced then New York police commissioner Roosevelt to shutter the city's brutal "police poorhouses," and Hine's photos of juvenile factory workers drove a nationwide expansion of child labor laws. Later, Joe Rosenthal's 1945 shot of Marines raising the flag over Iwo Jima gave war-weary America the will to keep fighting, while Eddie Adams' famous 1968 photo of Vietnam's police chief executing a Vietcong terrorist—a decisive moment if there ever was one—had the opposite effect, hastening the wind down of an unpopular war. Eugene Smith's early 1970s photos of mercury pollution in Minamata, Japan, not only buoyed the victims' lawsuit but stimulated worldwide environmental awareness. And in 2004 a series of amateur photos of US jailers humiliating Iraqi prisoners flashed across the Internet, forcing the closure of Abu Ghraib prison and a reexamination of America's torture policy.

So over the last century and a half, photo-essays have proven their ability not only to document but to actually change the course of human events. If that's the case, shouldn't we ask, "What are the essential photo-essays of *our* time, the pictures that will spark public discourse and instigate the sort of real-world reform provoked by Riis, Hine, Adams and Smith?"

What Matters attempts to answer that question with eighteen important photo-essays by this generation's preeminent photojournalists. The pictures in these essays aren't necessarily the best photos ever made—this isn't a greatest hits album—but they poignantly address the big issues of our time: global warming, environmental degradation, AIDS, the global jihad, genocide in Darfur, the inequitable distribution of global wealth and other equally compelling challenges.

Photo-essays have the proven ability not only to document but also to change the course of human events.

> Photojournalism works best when it is personal and specific but still conveys a universal concept.

In an undertaking this ambitious, it is important to understand what the medium does best, and what it doesn't do very well at all. For some very important issues, photojournalism is not the best way to tell the story. Despite our best efforts, and excellent guidance from a dozen top photo editors from major publications, we could not find a great photo-essay about the institutionalized corruption of America's campaign finance system. It is a crucial meta-issue that affects many other issues, but it doesn't lend itself to pictorial exposition. Then there are other big stories—such as the so-called digital divide between information "haves" and "have-nots"—about which we felt sure we'd find great pictures. But we couldn't identify ten or twelve strong images to convey the story. The point is, we believe that all of the stories in this book are essential, but we also realize there are other stories, just as important, that are best told in other media.

Basically, photojournalism works best when it is personal and specific but still conveys a universal concept. The world's premier conflict photographer and *What Matters* contributor, James Nachtwey, puts it this way, "I do not want to show war in general, nor history with a capital H, but rather the tragedy of a single person." Not surprisingly, Nachtwey demonstrates a deep understanding of the nature of photojournalism. The best photojournalism is always personal and specific. That's why Gene Smith did not photograph pollution worldwide, but rather the devastating effects of one particular type of pollution—methyl mercury—on one very small Japanese fishing village. Nevertheless, people who saw Smith's story in *Life* magazine and in his subsequent book, *Minamata*, easily universalized the lesson. In the same way, *What Matters* presents very specific pictures of, say, the ecological, cultural and economic devastation of West Africa's Niger Delta in order to make much larger points about the pernicious effects of petroleum production and consumption worldwide.

What Matters also puts great photo-essays in context by pairing photographs with insightful commentary by some of the best writers, thinkers and experts in their fields. These essays provide a much richer understanding of their topics than could ever be gained from the photos alone. But unlike most magazines, newspapers and

STREET EXECUTION,
SAIGON. Photograph by
Eddie Adams, 1968

books, the photographs drive the story here, while the words explain their larger significance.

Here's another challenge: Brady, Riis and Hines created their groundbreaking photo-essays 100 to 150 years ago, when photography was still pretty exotic. Only a few trained technicians could operate the machinery, and photographs were still considered technological wonders.

But over the last 150 years, making pictures has become progressively easier and increasingly common. With the recent proliferation of digital point-and-shoots and cell-phone cameras, a significant proportion of young people in wealthier nations carry some sort of camera with them at all times. And to a greater or lesser degree, almost everyone can operate the equipment. Add to that the distributive power of the Internet, and you get a world awash in imagery—most of it pretty vacuous. These days imagery permeates our lives. It's practically wallpaper. And in our image-saturated

world, it's sometimes difficult to cut through the visual clutter and shake things up. In his introduction to *Minamata*, Smith lamented, "Photography is a small voice at best. Daily we are deluged with photography at its worst—until its drone of superficiality threatens to numb our sensitivity to the image." Since Smith published his book in 1972, the problem has increased exponentially.

But certain photographs are still crucial. As *What Matters* contributor and climate change guru Bill McKibben says in his essay, "*Theoretical* is the word that people in power use to dismiss anything for which pictures do not exist. It is the reason we don't see shots of coffins coming back from Iraq; it's the reason the only prison abuse we really know about was at Abu Ghraib. Without pictures, no uproar; not in a visual age."

So in McKibben's words, *What Matters* contains images that will create uproar. And as such, many of the pictures in this book are pretty challenging. Some of them will make you cry; others will make you sick; and many of them will make you angry . . . which

If we show you these photographs, we believe that you will react with outrage… create an uproar…take action.

is our intent. We believe that modern-day hero-photojournalists such as Sebastião Salgado, Jim Nachtwey, Ed Kashi, Tom Stoddart and Stephanie Sinclair create photo-essays that can actually grab the world's attention; that their photographs are so transcendent, so compelling, if we show them to you, you will react with outrage . . . and create an uproar. And if you do want to take action, *What Matters* provides a menu of resources, web links and effective actions you can take to help right now. If, on the other hand, you look at these grim stories and think: "What's the use? The world is irredeemably screwed up," it is good to remember that we actually did abolish slavery and child labor in the United States; we abolished apartheid in South Africa; we defeated the Nazis; we pulled out of Vietnam; and Minamata Bay was eventually cleaned up. As the saying goes, "All great social change seems impossible until it is inevitable." So please look at these photographs. Read the words. And then, if the spirit moves you, do something . . . even something small . . . to help repair the world.

Meltdown
A Global Warming Travelogue

PHOTOGRAPHER
GARY BRAASCH
inside an ice
cave on the edge
of the Marr Ice
Piedmont, Anvers
Island, Antarctica.
The cave report-
edly has since
disappeared
as the glacier
retreated.

FOR A LONG TIME—THE FIRST FIFTEEN YEARS THAT WE KNEW about global warming and did nothing—there were no pictures. That was one of the reasons for inaction. Climate change was still "theoretical," the word that people in power use to dismiss anything for which pictures do not exist. It is the reason we don't see shots of coffins coming back from Iraq; it's the reason the only prison abuse we really know about was at Abu Ghraib. Without pictures, no uproar; not in a visual age.

But now the pictures have started to come, and they will not cease. Some show people: airlifted off the roofs of their houses in New Orleans' Lower Ninth Ward in the mad wake of Katrina, staring at their houses crumbling into the sea on the Alaskan coast, watching their graveyards flood on South Seas islands. Some show the massive power of nature, made more massive by our injection of chemicals into the atmosphere: walls of flame crashing up Southern California hillsides, enormous waves breaking over Mississippi seawalls. Some are almost clinical: the bathtub rings around drying reservoirs as evaporation takes its course. And some have the stately,

by **BILL McKIBBEN**
photographs by **GARY BRAASCH**

COAL YARD, INNER MONGOLIA. China adds a new coal-burning power plant large enough to power Dallas or San Diego every seven to ten days.

cold precision of the really big view: the satellite pictures, for instance, that show the steady melt of the sea ice above the Arctic Ocean. (They are like the before-and-after pictures from some makeover gone horribly wrong, the beautiful world disfigured by some out-of-control plastic surgeon.)

I think that these pictures—many of them taken by Gary Braasch, who has chronicled this crisis more relentlessly than anyone else with a camera—will someday be the iconic images of our decade, even more than the shots of the Twin Towers aflame, because they presage the images we will spend this century viewing—on our screens, and out our windows. They are the opening shots of a movie that will keep playing, with horrible relentlessness, for all our time on earth. It's possible we'll have more terrorist attacks—but it is not possible that they will pose the same threat to our civilization and to our planet as the steady horror now unfolding in what we used to call the natural world. This is what the earth looks like now.

Some things, of course, don't show up in pictures. To really understand what's going on, you need a split screen. On one side,

there would be Tuvaluans in their sinking shacks, Bangladeshis in their flooding paddy fields, Inuits on their crumbling shores; on the other side, some Ford, GM and Toyota ads for monster SUVs. When we say that this is a man-made crisis, we don't mean all men. We mean those of us, of both genders, who inhabit the rich world—Americans make up 4 percent of the population but produce 25 percent of the world's carbon dioxide. Even the Chinese, who have begun to burn lots of coal, can't compare—that country's emissions matched ours in the past year, but there are four times as many people there. And we've been doing it for a hundred years. This one's on us.

You would also need a picture that somehow sums up the forces that keep us from doing anything about climate change. A stack of forty billion one-dollar bills 10,856 miles high might do—that's how much profit ExxonMobil made in 2006, more profit than any other corporation in the history of corporate profits. It takes but a small fraction of that haul to buy the political juice that keeps Congress from acting responsibly.

US SCIENTISTS explore the face of the receding Marr Glacier, near Palmer Station, Anvers Island, Antarctica.

But there are other iconic images emerging too, and some of them are much happier. Take the wind turbine, now the universal symbol for a future of green progress: those huge blades spinning slowly against the Danish countryside, the German hills, the North Sea coast—maybe soon against the backdrop of Cape Cod or the ridges of Vermont, if the opposition can be overcome (opposition rooted at least in part in an old set of iconic images of "unspoilt nature"). The breeze made visible, in a giant white wheel slowly turning from past to future.

And better yet are the pictures that show people rallying to the planet's defense—a kind of immune system finally starting to kick in, hopefully before the sickness is too far gone. I've been thinking a lot about pictures like that, as I've made the transition from writer to activist. In early 2007, six college kids and I decided to see if we could launch a large-scale protest movement in the United States. We set up a Web site, stepitup07.org, and started sending out e-mails asking people if they would organize protests twelve weeks hence. We had no budget and no organization, but we soon found a deep stratum of people across America haunted by global warming and eager to do something about it. Before many weeks had passed, they had organized 1,400 separate rallies in all fifty states, the biggest day of grassroots environmental protest since the first Earth Day in 1970.

We thought long and hard about how to make the most effective use of those rallies. And our answer was: pictures. We asked every organizer to upload a photo of their rally to our Web site before the big afternoon was out. And we encouraged them to think in visual terms.

By nightfall, we had a collage of images from across America. There was an underwater demonstration off Key West—scuba divers hoisting signs in front of a coral reef that, like all its cousins around the world, will be destroyed unless we can bring the heating of the seas under control. In lower Manhattan there were thousands of people in blue shirts holding hands and forming a "sea of people" to show where the tideline will fall across some of earth's most expensive real estate once seas start to rise. On the glaciated peaks of the far West (which won't be glaciated much longer, as Braasch's pictures here make clear), alpinists made multiday ascents and then

Top:
HOUSES IN THE SHADOW
of the Amos coal-fired power plant in Poca, West Virginia.

Bottom:
CHINA STEEL PLANT,
part of Shougang Group, a major coal-burner.

AERIAL VIEW OF SMOG over
Chicago during a record heat wave.

We have eight
more years to reverse
the flow of carbon
into the atmosphere, or
else we will soar past
the red lines that guard
the stability of the
great ice shelves.

**CLIMATE CHANGE
RESEARCHERS** witness
the breakup of the Müller
Ice Shelf on the Antarctic
Peninsula.

The next few years are a final exam for the human species. Does that big brain really work or not?

skied down in formation, webcasting as they went. There were pictures from church steps and farm fields, California beachfronts and Louisiana levees, young people, old people, people of all kinds.

In fact, one of the very best pictures actually arrived at our Web site weeks early. It came from the Alpha Phi sorority chapter at the University of Texas at Austin, and it showed 180 sorority women—with the broad smiles one would expect of Lone Star lasses—holding a sign with our demand: Step It Up Congress: Cut Carbon 80% by 2050. They attached a note to the bottom: "We wanted to show it wasn't just the hippies who cared." That was both sweet and insightful. It's hippies who start things—the kind of people who see the change that's needed a little earlier than the rest, who don't require the photographic proof in hand to start thinking subversive thoughts. But it's sorority chapters and Chambers of Commerce and evangelical congregations who finish things off, move them into the political mainstream where they can't be ignored. These are steadier folk, and they rightly ask for some evidence—evidence that we now can provide to all in great abundance. Al Gore's documentary, *An Inconvenient Truth*, provided the first of those images to really make a deep impression, but now they appear every night. It's why polling shows that 70 percent of Americans understand the problem and want government to act. It's the reason there's some hope.

But that hope sits uneasily against the scale of the problem. This is a social issue unlike any other we've ever faced. It's not like the civil rights movement, much as we need a campaign as morally urgent and as passionate as that great uprising. The civil rights movement knew it would triumph—it knew it would go through hell, but it knew it would emerge. As Martin Luther King Jr. said almost every time he spoke, "The arc of the moral universe is long, but it bends toward justice." He knew eventually they'd win.

But we don't have eventually. We have only now. Our greatest climatologist, James Hansen, has given us eight more years to reverse the flow of carbon into the atmosphere, or else soar past the red lines that guard, among other things, the stability of the great ice shelves above Greenland and the West Antarctic. (If you want to imagine pictures of the future—well, there's 25 feet of sea level rise

in the ice above Greenland alone. Twenty-five feet!) Can we change that fast? It's not at all clear that we can.

In fact, the one thing that is clear is this: the next few years are a kind of final exam for the human species. Does that big brain really work or not? It gave us the power to build coal-fired power plants and SUVs and thereby destabilize the working of the earth. But does it give us the power to back away from those sources of power, to build a world that isn't bent on destruction? Can we think, and feel, our way out of this, or are we simply doomed to keep acting out the same set of desires for MORE that got us into this fix?

At some level, the answer depends on our imaginations. We can and will dream up new technologies—we already have the wind-mill and the solar panel and the bicycle, all of which would help immensely. But we need a picture in our minds of the world to come—a picture that shows a world more balanced, less careening. A world of farmers markets and trains, a world where 10 percent don't live high and 90 percent live low. A world almost, but not quite, beyond imagining.

THE PASTERZE GLACIER in the Austrian Alps, in 1875 (top) and 2004 (bottom). The glacier has melted back nearly two miles (three kilometers).

THE ATHABASCA GLACIER in Jasper National Park, Canada, in a 1917 photograph by the A. O. Wheeler Survey of Boundary (top) and again in 2005 (bottom).

IN EARLY 2008, after years of drought, the water level of the Lake Powell reservoir in Arizona and Utah was at only 46 percent of capacity. Dangling Rope Marina, seen here in 2005, faces an uncertain future in one of the lake's disappearing channels.

TUVALU, a low-lying island nation north of Fiji, is threatened by rising sea levels.

GARY BRAASCH

Gary Braasch (US) is a recipient of the Ansel Adams Award for Conservation Photography and a fellow of the International League of Conservation Photographers. He has created assignments and portfolios on environmental issues since 1980 and has methodically documented the visible effects of global warming since 1998. His photographs have been published by the United Nations and have appeared in *Time*, *Discover*, *Audubon*, *National Wildlife*, *Smithsonian*, *Scientific American*, *Natural History*, *Nature* and *National Geographic*. Braasch's fourth book, *Earth under Fire: How Global Warming Is Changing the World*, was published in 2007.

BILL MCKIBBEN

Bill McKibben (US) is the author of a dozen books on the environment, most recently *The Bill McKibben Reader*, a collection of his essays. A former staff writer at *The New Yorker*, McKibben wrote *The End of Nature*, the first book for a general audience about climate change. A scholar in residence at Middlebury College, he has worked with students to organize 2,000 demonstrations against global warming in recent years.

WIND TURBINES alongside a dike in Flevoland. The Netherlands, partially built on land reclaimed from the sea, is in the forefront of the offensive against global warming and rising sea levels.

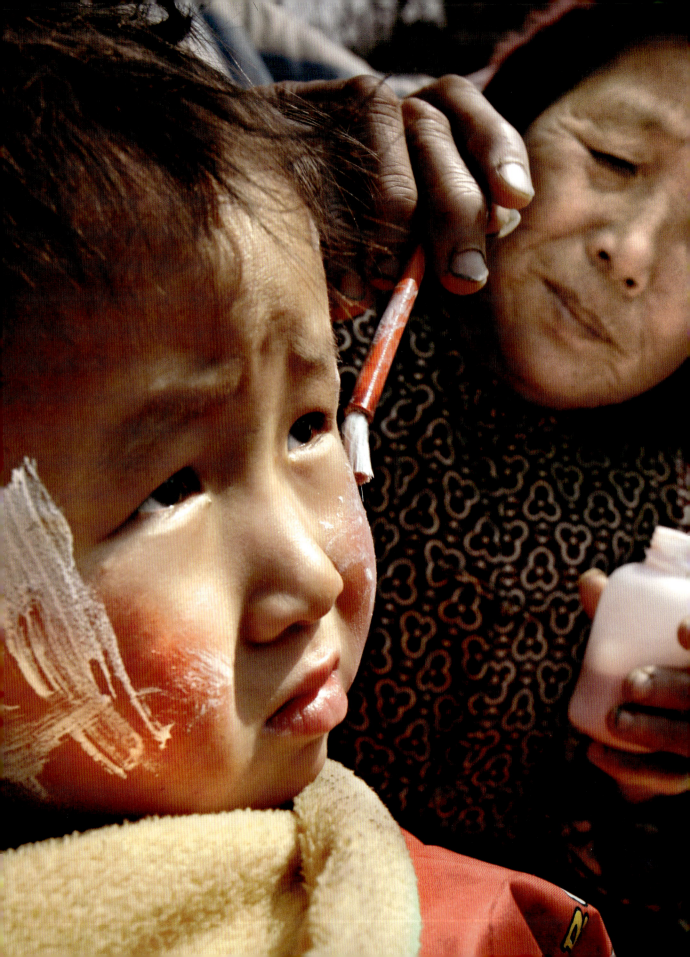

ECONOMIC MIRACLE, ENVIRONMENTAL DISASTER

The Degradation of the Huai River Basin

DECADES OF EXTRAORDINARY GROWTH have catapulted China to the top of the world's economic charts, earning the admiration of much of the rest of the world. Indeed, China's continued economic rise has been one of the few certainties of the twenty-first century. Increasingly, however, the China story is not one of economic miracle but of environmental disaster.

Worries over air quality at the Beijing Olympics, tainted products and China's rapidly growing contribution to global climate change have focused international attention on the environmental downside of China's growth. At home, the Chinese people watch as environmental degradation and pollution transform their

by **ELIZABETH C. ECONOMY**
photographs by **STEPHEN VOSS**

JIA JIALE'S grandmother applies lotion to treat rashes that appeared when she moved to Sunying, in China's Huai River Basin.

Top:
DEBRIS AT THE BASE of
a pipe that releases black
water from the state-owned
Lianhua MSG factory. Local
villagers protested when
many became sick with
stomach and intestinal
ailments. In 2004, Lianhua
("Lotus Flower") provided
clean tap water to the village,
but the company continued
to pollute the river.

Bottom:
A TRASH DUMP
in Shenqiu County clogs
streams and pollutes
the groundwater.

Following pages:
WASTEWATER FLOWS from
a pipe at the state-owned
Lianhua MSG factory. Lianhua
is the largest producer of
MSG in China and one of
the largest polluters in the
Huai River Basin.

landscape, and in the process endanger their health and future livelihoods. No one is exempt from the environmental consequences of China's brand of unfettered economic development, but as Stephen Voss' pictures so heartbreakingly illuminate, China's poorest are particularly vulnerable.

In China's cities, merely walking out the front door results in an immediate assault on the senses. The Chinese people complain most often about noise pollution. A cacophony of construction booms and car horns is a permanent fixture of life. The sky is often blanketed in a thick gray haze of pollutants. The culprits are the ever-present coal-fired power plants and giant heavy-industry complexes that fuel the country's growth, and more and more the noxious emissions of automobiles. The Chinese are in the midst of an American-style love affair with private cars. The country is adding 14,000 new cars to its roads every day and is in the process of laying 52,000 miles of new roadways—10,000 more miles than the entire US interstate highway system. By 2030, China is expected to surpass the United States as the country with the most cars on its roads.

More broadly, Chinese consumption patterns are also following those of the West, despite the warnings of prominent Chinese cultural and environmental leaders. The country's moneyed city dwellers desire air conditioners, refrigerators and second homes. Popular leisure activities for the wealthy include carbon-intensive activities such as yachting, golfing and car clubs. In the process, urban residents consume 350 percent more energy than rural Chinese, and more than 70 percent of this energy comes from dirty-burning coal. Every seven to ten days, another coal-fired power plant, big enough to serve all the households in Dallas or San Diego, opens somewhere in China. The environmental toll is enormous. China has five of the world's ten most polluted cities, and on an average day in China's major cities, 75 percent of the residents are breathing unclean air. The end result: 750,000 Chinese die prematurely every year from air pollution–related respiratory diseases.

For all their wealth, China's cities have yet to conquer the challenge of clean water. Among all of China's 660-odd cities, only one small city of 200,000, Lianyuan in Hunan Province, can claim

THE WATER TREATMENT FACILITY of the Lianhua MSG factory.

to provide clean drinking water straight from the tap. In the rest of the country—even the country's capital, Beijing—residents boil their water or buy it in bottles. Even then, they have no real assurance that the water is safe to drink. And in this desperately water-scarce country, the urban infrastructure does little to conserve. Urban China loses up to 20 percent of its water through leaky pipes. Cities such as Shanghai and Tianjin have sunk six feet over the past decade and a half as precious underground water reserves are drawn down, causing skyscrapers to tilt and encouraging coastal flooding. Yet tilting skyscrapers are the least of the cities' concerns. In Beijing, factories, buildings and underground pipelines have all been destroyed by the plundering of underground aquifers and the resultant land subsidence.

The environmental costs levied on China's 400 million urban residents pale in comparison, however, to those faced by the country's more than 800 million farmers and other rural residents. Much of China's countryside suffers from severe land degradation, the result of centuries of deforestation and poor land management. Today, China—which is roughly the same size as the United States—is almost one-quarter desert, and the desert is advancing at more than 1,300 square miles, approximately the size of the state of Rhode Island, each year. Entire villages in China's north have been lost, submerged in sand by the encroaching desert. The country's State Forestry Administration estimates that desertification affects 400 million Chinese, many of whom lose the ability to farm their land or graze their animals and join the ranks of the tens of millions of internal environmental refugees, who often migrate to the big cities in search of new homes and jobs.

Rural Chinese must also contend with a dire water situation. The small-scale industries that have sprouted throughout the countryside pollute with impunity. As Voss' photographs illustrate, pulp and paper, tanning, chemical and other factories set up shop along the banks of China's rivers and simply dump their waste into the water. Often the factories are protected by local officials who have a financial stake in their survival. More than a quarter of the water that flows through China's seven major river systems and their tributaries is unfit even for industry or agriculture, much less human consumption. The Yellow River, one of the world's longest, supplies water to more than 150 million people and 15 percent of China's agricultural land. Yet two-thirds of its water is considered unsafe to drink, and 10 percent is classified as sewage. In 2007, Chinese officials announced that over one-third of the fish species native to the Yellow River had become extinct due to damming or pollution.

Such alarming statistics beget other even more alarming numbers. Nearly 700 million people drink water contaminated with animal and human waste, and according to the country's Ministry of Water Resources, 190 million Chinese drink water so contaminated that it makes them sick. It doesn't help that an estimated two-thirds of China's rural population lacks access to piped water—a development failure that has become one of the leading causes of

Some 190 million Chinese drink water so contaminated that it makes them sick.

China is adding 14,000 new cars every day and is laying 52,000 miles of new roadways—more than the entire US interstate system.

death among children under the age of five. Local economies also suffer when villagers can't sell their grain or eat the crops planted along the river because the water is so polluted. As much as 10 percent of China's farmland is believed to be polluted, and each year 12 million tons of grain are contaminated with heavy metals absorbed from the soil.

China's environmental challenge moves well beyond simply the problems faced by any society at the height of its industrialization. The lack of transparency, official accountability and rule of law that defines China's authoritarian political system makes protecting the environment particularly difficult. Perhaps no project better exemplifies this challenge than the Three Gorges Dam. After decades of promoting the virtues of the dam—the largest in the world—Chinese officials are only now beginning to acknowledge the dam's failures. The potentially negative consequences of the dam, including dramatically rising levels of water pollution, deadly landslides, loss of species and relocation of millions of Chinese, were all known to those involved in the planning of the dam for decades, yet open discussion was forbidden. A journalist, Dai Qing, was imprisoned for ten months for her efforts to air publicly the dam's likely costs and benefits. Now that the dam has contributed to the death or homelessness of thousands and there is talk of relocating three to four million more Chinese, the price of silence has become clear. Yet still, the Chinese government refuses a fully honest and open assessment of the situation.

The Chinese people increasingly have little patience for official obfuscation and corruption. Journalists push to report honestly on pollution disasters, and lawyers bravely take cases on behalf of pollution victims. When confronted with poisoned water and air, sick children, and ruined crops, the Chinese people sometimes simply take to the streets. There are more than 50,000 environmental disputes in China every year. For example, in 2006, the residents of six neighboring villages in the poor interior province of Gansu held repeated protests over a six-month period against zinc and iron smelters that they believed were poisoning them. Fully half of the 4,000 to 5,000 villagers exhibited lead-related illnesses ranging from vitamin D deficiency to neurological problems. In 2007,

when local officials in southern China illegally confiscated farmers' land to construct a power plant, there were violent demonstrations. In the cities, where education levels are often higher and information flows more freely, Chinese citizens have even begun to protest in advance of a potential environmental threat. In 2007, for example, Beijing residents protested a proposed waste incinerator, and the people of the coastal city of Xiamen marched by the thousands, successfully halting the planned construction of a petrochemical plant near the city center.

As pressure on China's leaders mounts from below, the rest of the world is also increasingly impatient with the country's failure to turn its environmental situation around. Pollutants that build up and threaten China's ecosystem and the health of its people also traverse the Pacific and affect the United States and other countries. China's contribution to global climate change will soon dwarf that of the rest of the world. The country already ranks as the world's largest importer of illegally logged timber and the biggest polluter of the Pacific Ocean.

THE VILLAGE of Huangmengying received national attention when the Chinese media publicized its soaring cancer rates. The government shipped in bottled water for Huangmengying but offered little help to other similarly affected villages.

LIU TIANHENG, who has stomach cancer, examines his X-ray at the Shenqiu County Hospital.

WANG SHIWEU, 42, is an accountant by training but now dispenses traditional Chinese medicine in Huangmengying. Most villagers are no longer able to afford conventional treatment for their cancer.

China's leaders are well aware of the crisis they confront. The environment has moved to the top of their political agenda, and they have promised increased environmental investment, set impressive targets for reducing pollution and launched grand-scale campaigns to address particularly challenging problems of environmental degradation. International environmental nongovernmental organizations and their counterparts in China are working aggressively to provide grassroots support for environmental protection. A number of multinational corporations have even adopted environmental protection as an important and integral part of their business ethic in China. Public pressure from around the world counts in Beijing.

Yet the situation continues to deteriorate. Rapid growth remains the priority for many in Beijing, and certainly for most local officials. Hundreds of millions of Chinese still live in relative poverty; per-capita GDP amounts to less than US$2,000 annually.

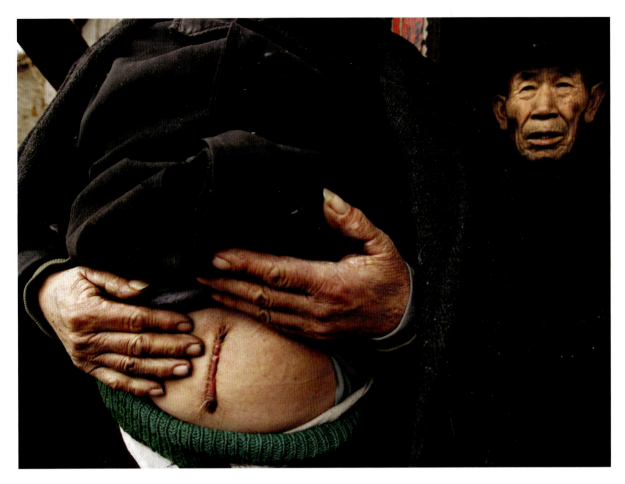

In such an economic environment, the up-front costs of environmental protection can appear daunting, particularly for officials in the less-developed interior of the country with far fewer economic resources. And there are few incentives for local officials to put the environment first. Moreover, opening the political space to allow for greater citizen involvement in environmental protection—through a free media, unregulated nongovernmental organizations or an independent judiciary—is seen as too politically risky by most Chinese Communist Party officials, whose primary concern is maintaining power. Yet only this type of fundamental reform of the country's political economy will yield the environmental improvements the Chinese leaders and people desire. In the meantime, local economies will suffer, people's health will deteriorate, social unrest will grow and the China story may, in the end, change from economic miracle to environmental collapse.

WANG ZI QING, 60, shows the scar where a tumor was removed from his stomach. He was a fisherman but is now too sick to work. His two brothers died from cancer within a month of each other. Wang blames polluted groundwater.

STEPHEN VOSS

Stephen Voss (US) is a Washington, DC–based photographer whose work has been featured in many international publications, including *Time*, *The Atlantic*, *The New York Times*, *Newsweek*, *Forbes*, *Der Spiegel* and *Condé Nast Portfolio*. He received a Creative Visions Foundation grant to document homelessness in Portland, Oregon, and photos from the project were featured in a national exhibit. Voss' recent work includes photo-essays on US Superfund sites and international adoption. His documentary work focuses on US politics and on environmental and globalization issues worldwide.

ELIZABETH C. ECONOMY

Elizabeth C. Economy (US) is the C. V. Starr Senior Fellow and director for Asia Studies at the Council on Foreign Relations. Economy is the award-winning author of *The River Runs Black: The Environmental Challenges to China's Future* (2004). Her op-ed pieces and book reviews have been published in *The New York Times*, *The Washington Post*, *The International Herald Tribune*, *The Boston Globe*, *Newsday* and *The South China Morning Post*. Her forthcoming book discusses how China's resource quest is changing the global political, environmental and economic landscape.

CHILDREN PRACTICE
English at a school in the village of Sunying, where more than eighty people have died from cancer since 1990.

THIRSTY WORLD

The Desperate Everyday Quest for Safe Water

WOMEN AND CHILDREN are responsible for hauling water in Africa. This four-year-old girl in Ghana walks two-and-a-half miles (four kilometers) twice each day to fetch buckets of water for her family.

WATER IS THE KEY TO LIFE. It is fundamental to all human activities. Water grows the food we eat, generates the energy that supports our modern economies and maintains the ecological services on which we all depend. Yet billions of people worldwide still lack access to the most basic human right: safe, clean, adequate water.

As you would expect, the vast majority of these people are among the poorest in the world, living in sub-Saharan Africa and southern Asia. Brent Stirton's images tell many stories if you know how to read them—from the tragedy brought by lack of safe water or too much water, to the joy and life-changing effects that a new water system can offer.

Modern society began to flourish only when humans figured out how to deliver reliable water supplies to larger and larger concentrations of people, and how to remove the accumulations of waste that cities produce, thus reducing outbreaks of water-related diseases. Those services, which most of us take for granted, are still pipe dreams for vast populations in the poorest places on the planet.

by **PETER H. GLEICK**
photographs by **BRENT STIRTON**

BANGLADESH FLOODS
for months at a time during the monsoon season. Its location on the floodplains of both the Ganges and the Brahmaputra rivers makes it one of the most flood-prone regions on earth.

This failure to meet the basic human need for water has direct, tangible and unacceptable consequences: drink dirty water and you get sick. Witness the father caring for his son afflicted by a guinea worm parasite. See the girl wasting away from cholera. Look at the consequences of arsenic poisoning on Bangladeshi villagers. And know that all of these diseases are completely preventable.

More than half the population of our modern, "civilized" world still suffers from water services inferior to those of the ancient Greeks and Romans. As a result, water-related diseases continue to be a serious problem in many parts of the world. Water-related diseases fall into several types or classes, but the three that are most clearly associated with the failure to provide safe water and sanitation are waterborne, water-washed and water-based diseases.

Waterborne diseases include those transmitted by drinking contaminated water, particularly contamination by pathogens from human excreta. These include most of the enteric and diarrheal diseases caused by bacteria, parasites and viruses. Waterborne diseases also include typhoid and more than thirty species of parasites that

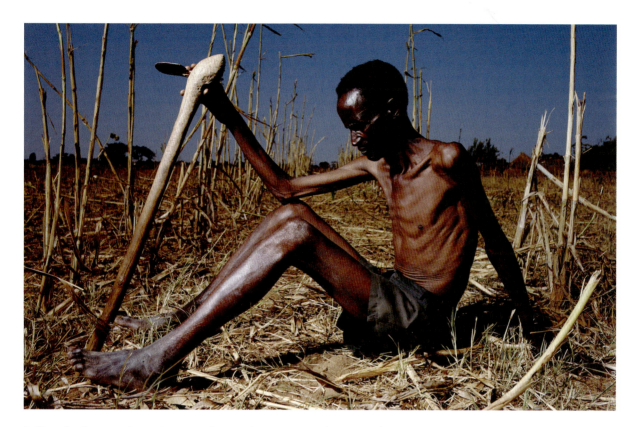

infect the human intestines. Evidence also suggests that waterborne diseases contribute to background rates of other diseases that are not detected or explicitly reported as outbreaks.

Water-washed diseases occur when there is insufficient water for washing and personal hygiene or when people wash with contaminated water. These include blindness caused by trachoma and diarrheal diseases passed from person to person.

Water-based diseases come from hosts that live in water or require water during part of their life cycle. These diseases are passed to humans when the hosts are ingested or come into contact with skin. The most widespread types are dracunculiasis, or guinea worm disease, in which a worm up to a meter long eventually and painfully emerges from the victim's skin; and schistosomiasis, a blood infection from a parasitic flatworm that causes chronic debilitation as well as liver and intestinal damage. Schistosomiasis, which currently infects 200 million people in seventy countries, is so prevalent in certain African and East Asian communities that the process of overcoming disease is considered an important rite of passage.

AS ZAMBIA ENTERED its sixth year of severe drought in 2003, this starving farmer sat among the ruins of his failed crop. He is HIV positive, and malnutrition accelerated the decline of his already weak immune system.

M uch of the
country lives
in constant fear
of either too
much water or
not enough.

Clean, safe water and sanitation have successfully eliminated most of these water-related pathogens in wealthier nations. But they remain a major concern in much of the developing world. According to the World Health Organization, there are on the order of 250 million cases of water-related diseases annually, excluding common diarrheal diseases. In 2000, the United Nations estimated there were more than four *billion* cases of diarrhea annually and more than two million deaths a year. Even these horrifically large numbers may be too small; the true extent of these diseases is unknown, and many cases of water-related illnesses remain undiagnosed and unreported.

Disease is only one consequence of the lack of safe water. Look at Stirton's photo of the little girl carrying a heavy load of water on her head. There is more to this than meets the eye. The girl is indeed "little"—she is four years old, and she is beginning what may be an entire childhood devoted to hauling water. She is not going to school. She won't learn how to be a leader in her community. She will be deprived of some of the most basic benefits of society—all because there is no local source of clean, reliable and safe water. Stirton photographed a girl, not a boy, because it is the girls who bear this burden throughout the developing world. And her burden is heavy, because water is heavy—eight pounds per gallon, a kilogram per liter.

My own work suggests that the minimum basic water requirement just for cooking, cleaning, drinking, bathing and simple sanitation is 50 liters per person per day—which means 50 kilograms, or more than 100 pounds of water, per person every day. Carrying just five gallons—enough for basic drinking and cooking alone—means carrying 40 pounds of water. Go outside and try to carry water now. Get a five-gallon container and carry it around the block where you live. It will open your eyes and strain your back. And five gallons is what disappears down the drain when you take a shower for two minutes—if you are using an efficient showerhead.

Even if girls do get to go to school, unless the school has water and sanitation, they spend much of the day not in class but hauling water to the school. And they often drop out at a young age rather

A CHILD PLAYS on a bamboo bridge over floodwater in Dhaka, Bangladesh. The floodwater is polluted and contaminated with waterborne diseases.

A FARMER AND HIS SON stand in the waters covering their crop fields on the outskirts of Dhaka.

O ur failure to provide safe water and sanitation will cause sickness, blindness, lost opportunities and, for a staggeringly large number of people, early death.

AN ELEVEN-YEAR-OLD GIRL in Ghana helps her blind mother and brother fetch water from a swamp. She has cared for them for six years, since they both lost their sight to trachoma, a bacterial infection of the eyelids linked to dirty water.

than face the prospect of puberty with no privacy, no sanitation and no proper hygienic facilities.

As with so many of the world's problems, Bangladesh often gets the worst of the water crisis, as Stirton's pictures suggest. Much of the country lives in fear of either too much water or not enough. Floods ravage the country during the monsoons, but inadequate or unsafe water supplies plague millions of villagers the rest of the year. Prior to the 1970s, most rural Bangladeshis relied on surface water ponds and shallow hand-pumped wells. But industrial effluents and poor or nonexistent sewage systems polluted this water, leading to millions of water-related diseases and deaths. The proposed solution was to dig nearly four million deep tube-wells to provide access to the presumably less-contaminated water table. And indeed, these wells helped reduce illness and death from cholera and dysentery. Overlooked, however, was the possibility that this groundwater could also be contaminated. But in the 1990s, more and more villagers began to be

Above:
SCARCE WATER in Tanzania often means competition between humans and animals.

Left:
SCHOOLGIRLS in Tanzania haul water on their way to school. Since the school has no running water, girls are sent out before, during and after class to fetch water from a well.

Right:
HIGH IN THE MOUNTAINS of Nepal near the Indian border, a man checks fog-harvesting nets, which collect water that is then stored in the village reservoir.

Far right:
NEPALESE WOMEN hike high into the mountains to fetch clean water from streams.

diagnosed with symptoms of toxic poisoning from naturally occurring arsenic. Bangladesh has now learned that millions of people may have traded one waterborne illness for another.

Getting people to change their drinking-water habits is hard: as Khushi Kabir, a Bangladeshi NGO director, said, "It took a long time to get people to use tube-well water, and it will take a long time to get them to change [again]." As if to underscore the challenge, Salim Uddin Mondal, a Bangladeshi villager, when told that his precious groundwater well was contaminated with arsenic, said, "If I die, I will die, but I will not go to fetch water from another man's house."

In a hydrologic quirk of fate, Bangladesh is also vulnerable to cataclysmic flooding, and Stirton has captured the pain and suffering that takes Bangladeshi lives and livelihoods. The risk of flooding will rise even further in Bangladesh as climate changes become more severe. Sea-level rise will increase the risk of tidal surges, while changing rainfall patterns and rapidly melting Himalayan glaciers will increase the risks of flooding along the region's major rivers.

Water also means food, and lack of water means lack of food. The poorest countries don't have sufficient infrastructure to buffer droughts or shortfalls of rain or runoff. This can mean the difference between enough food and death from starvation, weakened immune systems and competition over resources, as Stirton's poignant photo of a Zambian farmer so tellingly reveals.

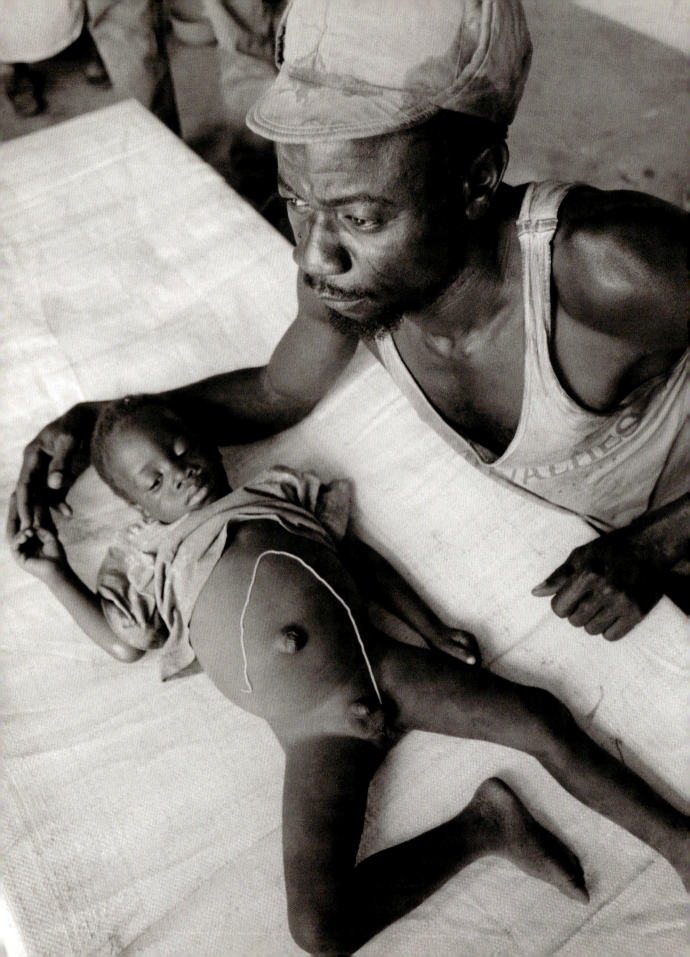

There are clear solutions to all of these problems, but new ideas, technologies, tools and, most importantly, concerted effort will be needed to provide universal access to safe, reliable and affordable water to the world's poor.

During the late twentieth century, traditional centralized water systems received most of the limited international funding given to water projects. While these systems often brought substantial benefits to many urban users, their high cost also meant that insufficient capacity could be built to satisfy all users and needs. And the technical complexity of these systems often meant that insufficiently trained personnel could not maintain operations. Throughout the developing world, we see the skeletons of expensive water systems that were built but never operated, or that operated briefly before failing.

In order to address the overall affliction of poverty, including unmet needs for basic water supply and sanitation, the United Nations and the international community announced the Millennium Development Goals (MDGs) in 2000. These included the goal of reducing by half the number of people unable to obtain or afford safe drinking water and sanitation by 2015.

Achieving the MDGs is a laudable objective, but even if they can be achieved, hundreds of millions of poor people will still lack basic water services. Moreover, we are more than halfway to the target date of 2015, and the levels of financial and institutional commitment to water issues have not been adequate. There now seems to be little chance that the MDGs will be met—particularly as they pertain to water. This must be considered one of the most serious public health crises we face, and it deserves far more attention and resources than it has received so far.

The price for our failure to provide universal safe water and sanitation will be paid by the poorest populations of the world in sickness, lost educational and employment opportunities, and, for a staggeringly large number of people, early death. This is morally unacceptable in a world that values equity and decency. But at present, it appears unavoidable unless we can muster the will and commitment to provide clean, safe water for all.

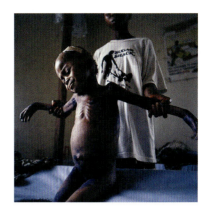

A YOUNG REFUGEE suffering from cholera is examined at a makeshift rural clinic in Buchanan, Liberia. In overcrowded refugee camps, human waste pollutes drinking water, spreading this infectious and sometimes fatal disease.

Left:
A GHANAIAN FATHER watches over his son as a guinea worm is slowly removed from the boy's scrotum. Guinea worms live in the mud around water holes and are ingested by people who drink infected water.

SOUTHERN MEXICO'S drought-stricken
Tehuacan Valley.

BRENT STIRTON

Brent Stirton (South Africa) is a senior staff photographer for Getty Images. He has photographed water issues in Zambia, Ghana, Sierra Leone, Tanzania, Liberia, Kenya, Madagascar, Bangladesh, Nepal, New Guinea and Mexico for five years. Stirton regularly works with the Global Business Coalition Against AIDS, the Global Fund Against AIDS, Tuberculosis and Malaria, the World Wide Fund for Nature, the Ford Foundation and the Clinton Foundation. He collaborated with CNN's Christiane Amanpour and Anderson Cooper to compile photo-documentaries on news events. Stirton has received four awards from the World Press Photo Foundation and three from the United Nations. His photographs have appeared in *Newsweek*, *National Geographic*, *CNN.com*, *The New York Times Magazine*, *The Washington Post Magazine*, *The London Sunday Times Magazine*, *Le Monde*, *Geo* and many other international publications.

PETER H. GLEICK

Peter H. Gleick (US) is cofounder and president of the Pacific Institute in Oakland, California, and an internationally recognized water expert. He was named a MacArthur Fellow for his work. Gleick's research and writing address the critical connections between water and human health, the hydrologic impacts of climate change, sustainable water use, privatization and globalization, and international conflicts over water resources. The BBC named Gleick a "visionary on the environment," and in 2006 he was elected to the US National Academy of Sciences. Gleick earned a BS from Yale and an MS and PhD from the University of California, Berkeley. He serves on the boards of numerous journals and organizations, and has authored many scientific papers and six books, including the biennial report *The World's Water*.

THE NEW WELL in this north Ghana village, made possible by the British NGO Water-Aid, means local women no longer have to walk long distances for water.

FALLOUT

The Enduring Tragedy of Chernobyl

THE CHILDREN'S HOME in Vesnova, Belarus, cares for 150 children with severe mental and physical disabilities. Although the cause of these disabilities is a matter of dispute, many such shelters receive support from international Chernobyl aid programs.

THE SITE FOR CHERNOBYL WAS CHOSEN IN 1970: in northern Ukraine, on the left bank of the Pripyat River, which links up through the Kyiv Reservoir to the Dnipro or Dnepr River, the Ukraine's main water supply. The first Chernobyl reactor came on line in October 1977. Three more followed in 1978, 1981 and 1983.

These graphite-moderated reactors, known as RBMKs (the Russian acronym for "high-power channel reactor"), experienced frequent problems from the start. Between 1981 and 1985 there were more than 381 emergency shutdowns at RBMK reactors in the Soviet Union, including more than 100 at the Chernobyl station itself. Most of these problems were blamed on faulty equipment, but there was also a well-known and fundamental problem: all RBMK reactors were built with more than thirty known flaws. Most seriously, they became unstable if operated at low power.

On the night of April 25, 1986, the Chernobyl control room crew ran an experiment on the fourth reactor unit to see how long a spinning turbine would continue to generate power after

by **DAVID R. MARPLES**
photographs by **GERD LUDWIG**

CHERNOBYL UNIT 4 is so radioactive that even workers in protective gear and respirators can stay inside for only fifteen minutes a day.

shutdown but before emergency turbines kicked in. The test was carried out by two inexperienced operators assisted by fifteen shift workers. Neither the plant director nor the chief engineer was present, and all emergency shutdown facilities were disengaged for the experiment. When an operator tried to raise the power of the reactor, it caused a surge that blew the roof off the fourth reactor unit. Radioactive debris reached a height of two-thirds of a mile, and an estimated 50-60% of the reactor core's iodine-131 and 20–50% of its cesium-137—the most dangerous radio-nuclides in terms of their possible impact on the population—eventually entered the atmosphere before the hole was plugged fifteen days later, more than tripling the entire world's level of background radiation. The initial explosion actually released only a few hundred kilograms of particles. The rest were disseminated by a graphite fire, a 700-degree Celsius blaze that oxidized the number four reactor's graphite insulation. The wind blew the radiation cloud to the northwest, raining major fallout onto Belarus, which was only six miles from the station. The graphite fire then spread to the roof of the third reactor unit.

Initially the Soviet Union, under its new general secretary Mikhail Gorbachev, tried to conceal the accident from the public. An April 28 Radio Moscow bulletin, acknowledging the accident and admitting two deaths, was issued only after nuclear workers in Sweden detected radiation on their shoes before entering the Forsmark nuclear station. They quickly deduced that an accident must have occurred in the USSR. More detailed reports appeared in the print media on April 29, three days after the disaster occurred, repeating the figure of two dead, but giving no other details.

In response, the Politburo set up an operating group under Soviet Ideology Secretary Yegor Ligachev and Prime Minister Nikolai Ryzhkov. Meanwhile, the graphite fire continued to burn, drawing fire crews from Pripyat and Kiev, 80 miles to the south. Helicopters dropped lead, boron and sand into the reactor to quash the inferno. Twenty-nine firemen and first-aid workers reportedly died on the scene in the first few days.

A RADIATION WORKER in the contaminated control room of Chernobyl's Unit 4, where a series of errors triggered a meltdown.

R adiation levels at the reactor site were 77,000 times the background norm.

Initially, the authorities designated an evacuation area with a 10-kilometer (6.2-mile) radius around the reactor. This included Pripyat, the town built for reactor workers, which had a population of 45,000 at the time of the accident, and Chernobyl, population 10,000. But for several days life in Pripyat continued as usual, and no health warnings were issued to local residents. Men went fishing, and at least two weddings were held outdoors. Then a government commission took control of the Chernobyl site and began evacuating residents. On May 2, a week after the accident, Secretary Ligachev and Prime Minister Ryzhkov flew to Chernobyl and promptly expanded the evacuation zone from 10 to 30 kilometers (18 miles). Some 60,000 people were evacuated between May 2 and 4, a week after the accident occurred. The most serious victims were transported to the specialized Moscow Clinic No. 6, while others were taken to hospitals in Kiev. By May 4, 1,882 people had been hospitalized, including 204 with acute radiation sickness. At that point, a change in wind direction led to a dramatic rise in background radiation in the much larger city of Kiev (population 2.5 million). By May 8, radiation levels at the reactor site were 77,000 times the background norm.

By late May, a month after the accident, the key priority was the construction of a temporary roof—dubbed the SARKOFAG — over the destroyed fourth reactor unit. Another grave concern was that dropping tons of fire-retardant materials on the graphite fire might push the reactor downward toward the water table, threatening a so-called China Syndrome, in which the molten reactor core would breach the barrier underneath it and flow downward unimpeded—theoretically to the center of the earth. So coal miners were brought in to build a thick concrete shelf beneath the reactor. Other priorities were the collection and burial of radioactive deposits—starting with the roof of units 3 and 4—and the removal of the so-called Red Forest, which was critically irradiated.

The government commission divided the contaminated sector into four zones based primarily on the amount of cesium-137 in the soil. First, a confiscated Closed Zone with more than 40 curies of cesium in the soil. Then the Zone of Alienation—an area of compulsory evacuation that contained 15 to 40 curies of cesium

and was expected to remain empty for several decades. This, in turn, was ringed by the Zone of Permanent Control, where the soil contained 5 to 15 curies, and residents had the right to evacuation if they so desired. Territories in the fourth ring, with 1 to 5 curies in the soil, were to be constantly monitored. But the zones were essentially arbitrary, since even a single farmer's field could fall into all four categories depending on where the measurement was made.

During April and May about 118,400 people were evacuated, but often to areas that fell beneath the path of the radiation cloud, so they subsequently had to be evacuated again. By 2000, more than 350,400 people had been evacuated, with the largest portion moved between 1991 and 2000. About 163,000 were evacuated from

NINETEEN YEARS AFTER the evacuation, kindergarten rooms in the nearby town of Pripyat remain empty.

ABANDONED HOMES in
Teremtsy are slowly
reclaimed by nature.

Ukraine, 135,000 from Belarus and 52,400 from Russian territories.

The cleanup operation eventually involved some 800,000 people and was conducted under appalling conditions. Terms of service in the Zone of Alienation were extended without warning; lifetime levels of radiation were exceeded at random; and overexposure to radiation was common, especially on the reactor roof. One problem was that there was too much radiation to measure. Geiger counters simply did not work above a level of 25 rems, but workers regularly remained in the radiation zone long after this level was reached. (In the United States, areas where a person receives more than 0.1 rem per hour are designated high-radiation zones.)

For the first month the main work was carried out by volunteers, who came from all parts of the Soviet Union. These volunteers were eventually replaced by military reservists but were not monitored for future health problems. That many of the volunteers

subsequently died seems a foregone conclusion, but that fact appears in no government reports or documents. The health data surrounding Chernobyl was classified, and once troops arrived, all casualties were attributed by the USSR Ministry of Defense to manufactured illnesses such as "vegeto-vascular dystonia." No one who fell ill or died during this period—including Ukrainian film director Volodymyr Shevchenko, who filmed in the area during the first days after the accident—was officially a victim of the Chernobyl accident.

By the spring of 1989, largely due to *glasnost* (the new Soviet government openness under Gorbachev), maps appeared in the Soviet media indicating that the area of radiation fallout was much broader than first reported. Hundreds of Soviet families, particularly in Belarus, abruptly discovered that they were living in a radioactive zone. Suddenly, three years after the accident, a panicky

A PACK OF WILD DOGS at the former nuclear research center in Orane, Ukraine, near the Chernobyl plant.

In northern and western Ukraine, the long-term impact of pollution from cesium, strontium and plutonium (which has a half-life of 24,000 years) will continue in virtual perpetuity.

public was afraid to eat local foodstuffs. But by that point, the damage was done: radioactive food had been delivered locally and nationally, and had even been exported. This combination of secrecy and distortions alienated many Soviet citizens from their government. Even the acclaimed Soviet report to the International Atomic Energy Agency in Vienna in August 1986 about the causes of the accident went no further than attributing the entire fiasco to human error, completely ignoring the well-known defects in RBMK-type reactors.

So what were the long-term effects of the Chernobyl disaster, as measured two decades after the event? Many of the grim consequences can be seen in Gerd Ludwig's haunting photographs shot in 2006, and they should serve as a bleak warning. But the statistics are equally grim: The Chernobyl meltdown devastated Ukraine and Belarus, radioactively contaminating 8 and 22 percent of the landmass, respectively, along with 25 percent of the forests in Belarus and a very large area of Russia, including the Smolensk and Bryansk oblasts. More than five million people still currently reside in areas with dangerous levels of cesium in the soil. In Ukraine, the long-term impact of pollution from cesium, strontium and plutonium (which has a half-life of 24,000 years) will continue in perpetuity.

In Belarus the most affected regions are in the southeast, especially Homel. Many villages there have been depopulated. Others subsist in abject poverty, but virtually no young people remain. The so-called Shelter that was built over the fourth reactor unit in the fall of 1986 began to erode in 2001, so it has become necessary for a US–Ukraine consortium to construct a new roof. Until that happens, the structure is still in danger of a partial collapse because the heavy reactor cap that was flung off by the explosion overhangs the reactor.

While the health impact of the Chernobyl disaster has clearly been momentous, the actual casualty levels may never be known. The official figure of less than fifty dead is not in any way credible. A so-called Chernobyl AIDS has reduced immunity to disease in the contaminated zone, where morbidity rates have risen significantly over the past twenty years. In the mid-1980s, 80 percent of children were reported "healthy" in the zones later affected by radi-

ation fallout. That figure is less than 20 percent today. In Belarus alone, 1.5 million people—more than 15 percent of the population—are under medical observation, including more than 330,000 children.

The so-called Chernobyl liquidators—the more than 800,000 mostly young workers and volunteers who put out the fire, built the Shelter and carted away the radioactive debris—have suffered a variety of ailments. Four years after the event, at least 5,000 were dead. At least two reputable sources have cited more than 10,000 dead within five years. Many committed suicide.

By December 2000, according to a report by the Belarusian authorities, 7.1 million people in territories of the former Soviet Union had been declared "victims" of the Chernobyl accident by the government. Of those, 4.5 million lived in contaminated regions; more than 600,000 were liquidators, and 350,400 were evacuees. Some 148,274 people were designated "invalids."

LUDMILA KIRICHENKO visits her former apartment in Pripyat.

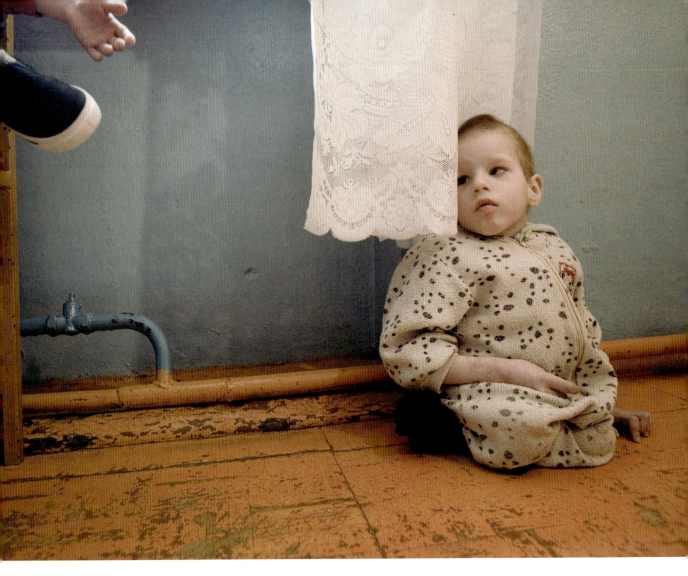

THE PSYCHO-NEUROLOGICAL
Boarding School for Children
in Novinki, Minsk, is a safe haven
for severely disabled children.

Although thyroid cancer was practically unknown in children before the Chernobyl disaster, it began to surface as a result of exposure to radioactive iodine-131. Some 5,000 children in affected areas have contracted this form of cancer. Although still within European norms, levels of leukemia have risen markedly throughout the contaminated zone. The increased frequency of previously rare diseases is often attributed by local doctors to radiation. Some scientists also cite an apparent link between radiation and the rise in newborn children with Down syndrome and other abnormalities. The first significant rise in this type of morbidity occurred only after the 1986 accident and is most prevalent in regions affected by Chernobyl fallout.

In 2000, the Ukrainian government closed the Chernobyl station permanently. But could more Chernobyl-type disasters occur?

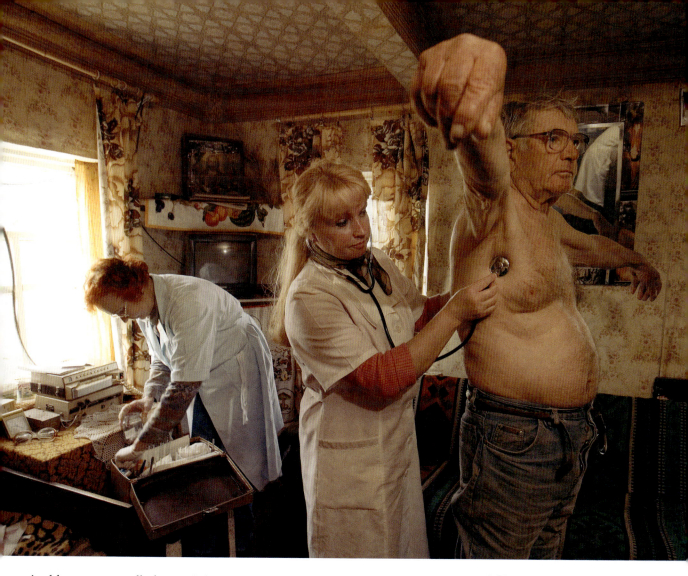

And have we actually learned the lessons of the tragedy? Apparently not. Only two decades after the Chernobyl meltdown, the affected countries have all made new commitments to nuclear power. Oil-rich Russia has embarked on a rapid nuclear expansion program; Ukraine relies on the atom for 40 percent of its energy needs; and Belarus, which lacks domestic oil and gas, has announced the construction of a new nuclear power station in the Mahileu region, an area already contaminated by Chernobyl. Post-Soviet safety levels remain minimal. And despite the presence of radioactive wastelands in northern Ukraine, southern Belarus and large swaths of territory in Russia, and notwithstanding the rapid spread of cancers, immune deficiencies and a health crisis among children in these former Soviet republics, in many respects the conditions that led to Chernobyl in the early 1980s are being repeated today.

A TEAM OF DOCTORS from Chernobyl Hospital makes monthly visits to elderly residents still living in the evacuation zone.

Following pages:
SUFFERING FROM THYROID CANCER, Oleg Shapiro, 54, and Dima Bognanovich, 13, receive care at the Thyroid Center in Minsk. As a "liquidator," Shapiro was exposed to extreme levels of radiation.

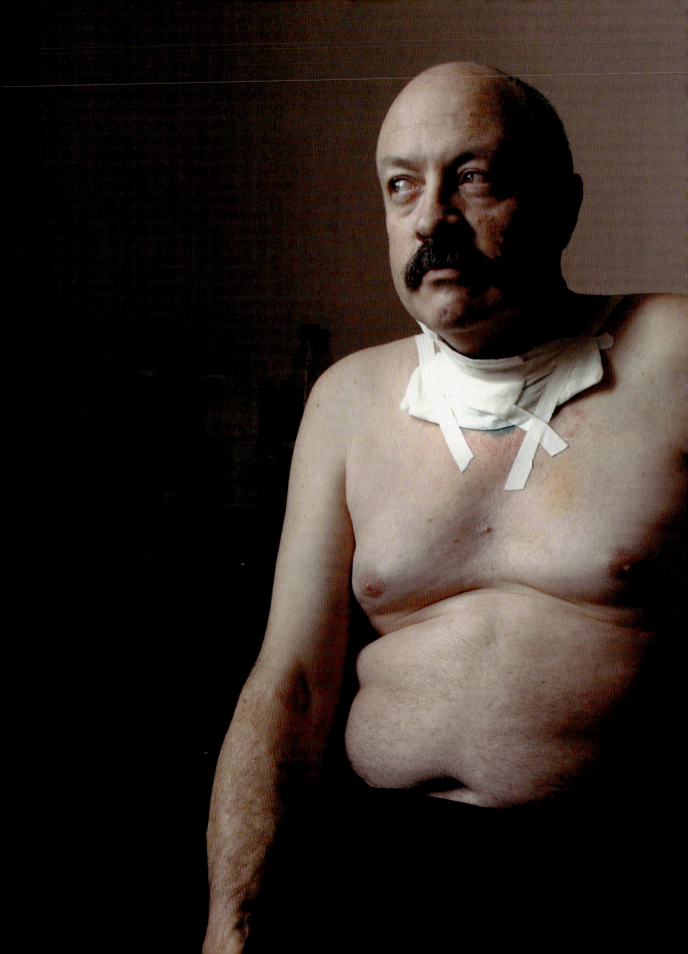

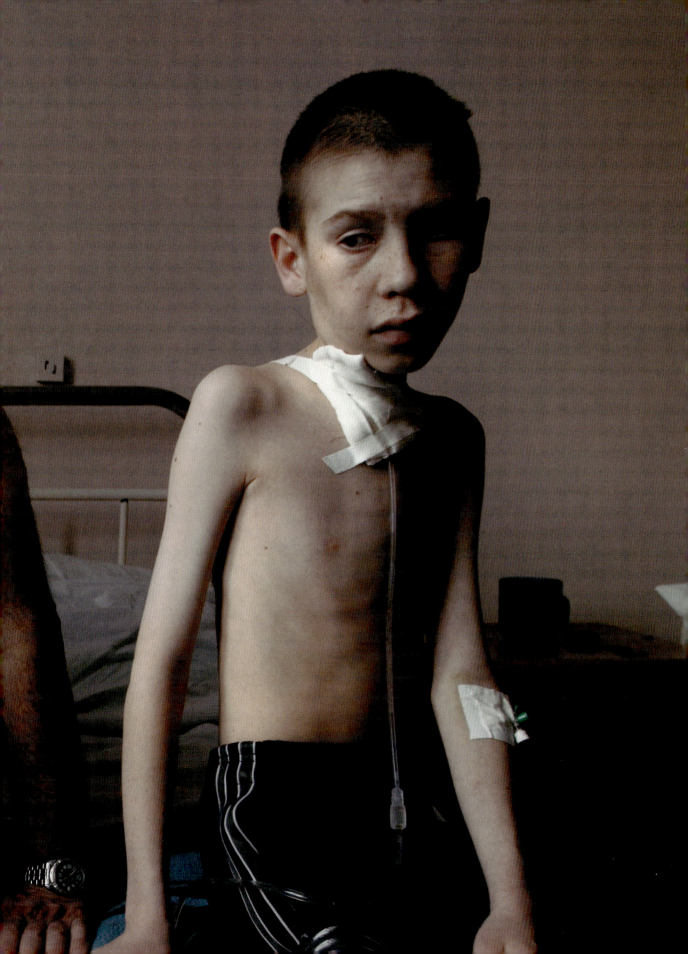

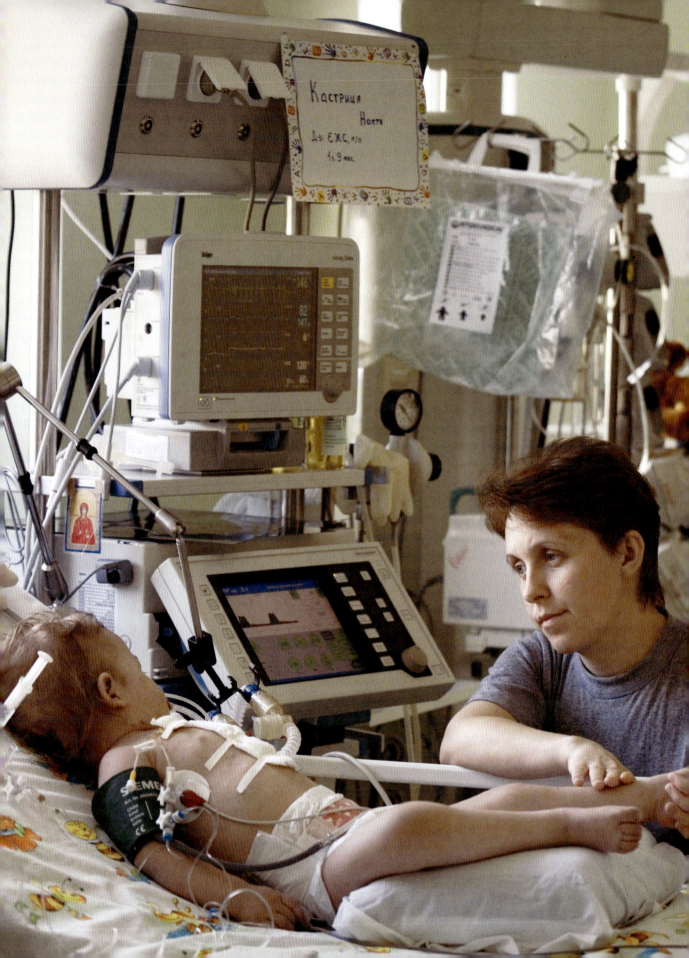

GERD LUDWIG

Gerd Ludwig (Germany) cofounded VISUM, Germany's first photographer-owned agency. He worked for *Geo, Stern, Spiegel, Zeit-Magazin, Time* and *Life* before moving to New York in 1984. In the early 1990s he became a contract photographer for *National Geographic*, focusing on social changes in Germany and eastern Europe. This culminated in his first book, *Broken Empire: After the Fall of the USSR*, a ten-year retrospective published by *National Geographic*. Ludwig is a veteran of the renowned *Day in the Life* book series and has won numerous awards, including the International Photography Association's 2006 Lucie Award as Photographer of the Year. Now based in Los Angeles, he has photographed in more than seventy countries. He lectures at universities and photographic workshops worldwide.

DAVID R. MARPLES

David R. Marples (Canada) is University Professor in the Department of History and Classics at the University of Alberta and director of the Stasiuk Program on Contemporary Ukraine at the Canadian Institute of Ukrainian Studies. He has authored twelve books, three of which concern the Chernobyl disaster, including *The Social Impact of the Chernobyl Disaster* and *Chernobyl & Nuclear Power in the USSR*. Marples serves as a consultant on Ukraine and Belarus on a regular basis for the government of Canada, the US Department of State and the Senate Foreign Relations Committee.

THE POST-OP department of the Children's Cardiological Center in Minsk. Here, local and international doctors help children born with a defect often called Chernobyl heart. In Belarus, only 15 to 20 percent of babies are born healthy.

Images of Genocide
How Should We Respond?

A MEMORIAL to the 1994 Rwanda genocide at the Church of Ntarama, in Kigali Province.

Photograph by Raymond Depardon

WHAT DO WE FEEL; WHAT DO WE THINK AND REMEMBER; how do we respond when we look at these haunting photographs from Rwanda, Cambodia, Bosnia and Kurdistan? These terrifying depictions of human suffering and brutality; these stark representations of inconsolable mourning and inanimate tools of destruction; these stunning, almost beautiful, breathtaking, strange yet strangely familiar frozen moments of what we know to be an eternity of loss and pain, of silent rage and shrieking hatred?

Photographs of horror can mobilize political and social action, especially when they evoke other, already familiar contexts that remind us of the consequences of inaction and the horror lurking behind still images. During the war in Bosnia, a single shot of emaciated men behind the barbed wire of a makeshift camp evoked worldwide recollections of Nazi concentration camps and triggered an outpouring of public outrage. Action did not follow right away, but

by **OMER BARTOV**
photographs by **MAGNUM PHOTOS**

public opinion began to build, putting pressure on governments.

Yet photographs can have precisely the opposite effect. Hundreds, nay, thousands of photographs from killing fields around the world often have only a numbing effect on the public. Over time, newspaper editors gradually push them to the back pages; then they do not publish them at all. Familiarity breeds indifference. Indeed, the ethnic cleansing in the former Yugoslavia was so heavily reported and so extensively photographed that it created a sense of overexposure and fatigue in the public. How much horror can we endure as we read our newspapers and watch television in our warm, cozy homes?

We might ask, for instance, what would have happened had CNN filed a report from Auschwitz in, say, July 1944, when the bulk of Hungarian Jewry was being exterminated there at an unprecedented rate with the most sophisticated industrial means available at the time? Would such reports have made a difference? Is the issue of passivity in the face of genocide one of secrecy, lack of knowledge, inability to comprehend and believe, as has so often been said about the Holocaust? Or is it, as contemporary mass killings in Africa and elsewhere indicate, not a matter of secrecy at all but rather a lack of political will and public interest? Does inundating the media with images have an effect similar to denying any coverage at all?

We know that the Vietnam War became unpopular because it was broadcast into American living rooms every night and, perhaps more crucially, because it ultimately necessitated a draft that threatened every young American male with the prospect of ending up in a body bag somewhere in the jungles of Southeast Asia. Taken together, that was incentive enough to protest.

But people protested about *Americans* going to, and dying in, Vietnam. The memorial wall in Washington, DC, is dedicated to *American* victims of a war in which far greater numbers of Vietnamese were killed by American weapons in American hands. Photographs of unknown people committing atrocities against yet another unknown group somewhere far away, using languages one doesn't speak and political rhetoric one cannot comprehend, are an entirely different matter.

Top:

THE MURAMBI GENOCIDE Memorial in Rwanda. In spring 1994, 5,000 Tutsis took refuge in a local school. They were discovered and massacred by Hutu extremists. Since then, 850 bodies have been exhumed, cured with lime, and displayed—a memorial to the more than 800,000 Tutsis killed by Hutus in one hundred days in spring 1994.

Photograph by Larry Towell

Bottom:

A MASS GRAVE found near Pilice, north of Sebrenica, Bosnia. The bodies are likely Muslims mass-murdered by Bosnian Croats.

Photograph by Gilles Peress

A 1991 SNAPSHOT shows Iraqi soldiers posing with the body of an executed Kurdish prisoner. The snapshot, re-photographed by Susan Meiselas, was removed from secret police files in Sulaimaniya, Iraq.

Photograph by Susan Meiselas

These photographs tell a truth we would rather not know. They have the power to take us to places we will never visit, show us sights we hope never to see. Yet they also become part of our vocabulary of images, linking in our minds different epochs and geographies, making connections between otherwise unrelated events, directing us to associate certain types of people with atrocity, bringing us closer to the site and at the same time distancing us from it. Africans, Balkan peoples, Jews—all are somehow linked in the mind to depictions of violence past and present.

But, at the same time, photographs tell us very little. We clearly understand the pain and suffering behind these photographs from Rwanda. But would we know whether the victims were Hutu or Tutsi without reading the captions? In fact, most of the approximately 800,000 victims slashed, mutilated and murdered in Rwanda during the 1994 genocide were Tutsi. But the bodies and bones we see here could just as easily be from the conflict now taking place in the Congo . . . or in the Ivory Coast.

It has been said that the public's overexposure to photographs of Jews victimized by the Holocaust created an association between Jews and victims; for some, it may even have provided a license for further violence against or even by Jews. Similarly, overexposure to photographs of suffering, mayhem, brutality and genocide in Africa can create an association between Africans and depravity, savagery and inhumanity, evoking stereotypes with long and insidious roots in the Western mind. And photos of atrocities in the Balkans might have ultimately triggered the collective European memory of that savage southeastern corner, long under Turkish Ottoman rule—a place of wild passions and "eternal hatred," an exotic and familiar yet inexplicable and explosive kind of hell with problems that can never be resolved.

In 1999, Germany was roiled by a debate over a traveling exhibition that presented more than 1,000 photographs of atrocities perpetrated by the German army on the Eastern Front during World War II. Many Germans were outraged to discover that contrary to what they had been told by their parents and grandparents, Nazi crimes were committed not only "behind the back" of the brave fighting troops but by their own relatives wearing the uniform of the Wehrmacht. When some critics pointed out that several photographs had been miscaptioned, there was a general sigh of relief: perhaps the entire exhibition was based on false premises. Indeed, photographs do not speak for themselves; they have to be contextualized. We need to know who is in the photo, how the situation came about and what subsequently happened. It is also helpful to know who took the photo, what the intended audience was and, if there is a caption, who wrote it. As it turned out, some of the photos in this exhibition showed both victims of the NKVD, the Soviet secret police, and victims of the Germans and their collaborators, who murdered the local Jews as punishment for their alleged support of the Soviets.

In much the same way, in 1945 a film was shown at the Nuremberg Military Tribunal that included extensive footage taken by the Allies when they liberated the German concentration camps. One scene in that film, in which piles of emaciated corpses are being bulldozed into a mass grave in Buchenwald, is strikingly similar to a photo by James Nachtwey depicting the burial of cholera epidemic victims in Zaire by French earth-moving equipment. In Nuremberg, this footage was used as evidence of Nazi atrocities against innocent Europeans and resistance fighters. The word *Jew* appears in the film only once. The genocide of the Jews played a secondary role in the trial, and the word *Holocaust* was not

Atrocity photographs, and even atrocity postcards, were sent home to family members as souvenirs.

Is there such a thing as a beautiful photograph of horror?

yet in use. But in 1961, the same footage was used during the trial of one of the Holocaust's chief architects, Adolf Eichmann, in Jerusalem, only this time as proof of the Shoah. The point is, it is all about context. Neither still photography nor documentary footage speaks for itself.

It is striking that only toward the end of World War II did journalists begin to feel that they had to rely on photographs to substantiate and illustrate their written descriptions of atrocities. Atrocity photographs were not new; such photos date back to the early days of photography. They were taken during the American Civil War, the early twentieth-century Balkan wars, World War I, the Armenian genocide of that period and the Rape of Nanking by the Imperial Japanese Army in 1937. Indeed, atrocity photographs, and even postcards of atrocities, often circulated among soldiers and were sent to family members as souvenirs. The snapshot of smiling Iraqi soldiers posing with an executed Kurd on page 86 is just such a souvenir.

Photographs of horror can be a source of pleasure or satisfaction, not only for people with a sadistic cast of mind but also for ordinary men and women immunized to the suffering of those they consider their enemies or inferiors. German soldiers marched into World War II equipped with cameras and took untold millions of photographs of the crimes they committed. Many of these photographs are still stowed away in attics and cellars throughout Germany, evidence of what came to be known as executionary tourism. Yet the official depictions of war, and the standards of journalism, were finally transformed only when the horrendous price of modern warfare, and the extent of organized, systematic inhumanity by genocidal regimes, was revealed in 1945.

Photographs, like paintings before them, can aestheticize violence, even atrocity, and many professional war and crime photographers are well aware of this danger. Is there such a thing as a beautiful photograph of horror? Fascism excelled in the aesthetics of violence, and we have no problem deploring this tendency. But it is also important to recognize that our own culture—with its free, often sensational press, and its predilection for violent movies and video games as entertainment—also threatens to numb our

Above:

THE 1993 AHMICI MASSACRE of Muslims by Croats in Bosnia.

Photograph by Gilles Peress

Following pages:

WRAPPED BODIES by a Rwanda roadside, 1994.

Photograph by Gilles Peress

WHEN THE KHMER ROUGE captured Phnom Penh in 1975, they expelled the city's residents to the countryside. The capital was deserted except for one school where Cambodian citizens were tortured, then either killed on the spot or transported to the killing fields. Khmer executioners photographed the detainees. The school, re-named the Tuol Sleng Prison Museum, displays these photos of some of the two million Cambodians who died in the genocide.

Photograph by Patrick Zachmann

sensibilities to actual suffering and to blur the distinction between virtual destruction and reality.

We have also witnessed the appearance of what have been called icons of extermination. There are a relatively small number of photographs, for instance, that are used whenever articles on the Holocaust appear in newspapers in Germany, Israel, France, the United Kingdom or the United States. We see naked women running to their deaths. We see a man sitting over a trench filled with bodies, smoking a cigarette. We see a child raising his hands in terror, a soldier with a rifle behind him. These photos have become visual shorthand for the Holocaust. They also dehumanize the victims and often contain a certain voyeuristic, pornographic quality. They show people about to be killed or turned into meaningless heaps of intertwined, indistinguishable limbs. They show the indifference or pleasure of the killers.

We see a group of young, handsome German soldiers laughing their heads off as they pull the beard of a tiny, elderly Jew. We wonder: Who took this photo? The photographer, too, may have ended up as a mutilated, frozen corpse in the Russian steppe. But such icons of inhumanity both record the deeds and potentially anesthetize us to them. At times they are so haunting, so terribly beautiful, that we can't take our eyes off them. We see a young, attractive mother, holding a baby; around her are other women in the process of undressing. It is December in Russia. We know they will soon be shot. We know that the photo must have been taken by a German policeman or soldier. But we cannot tear ourselves away from the black eyes looking straight at us. The photographs have no smell; they are silent; they are far away. They are there and we are here. We look at them, put them away and resume our daily routine.

For people looking at such photographs right after the war—the mountains of corpses, the endless piles of shoes, of hair, of children's prams, of artificial limbs stripped from bodies turned into ashes—the conclusion was clear: Never again! This became the slogan written on countless memorials erected throughout Europe in the wake of Nazi defeat. And this is why looking at these photographs of modern genocide is not only horrifying but also deeply depressing. Ultimately, all the high rhetoric of the postwar period

Iconic photographs of inhumanity both record the deeds and potentially anesthetize us to them.

came to naught. Never again? Are we as horrified today by these photos as the men and women of 1945 when they saw photographic evidence of genocide for the first time in their newspapers? Have we become inured to them? Is it less troubling for us to look at them because they depict Africans or Bosnians or Kurds?

Killings in Darfur, in the Congo and in so many other places around the world still go on. The photographs and documentaries expose the horror. The journalists explain; the politicians make excuses for inaction. Does it even matter whether the skeletons are Hutu or Tutsi? Even the killers were not sure at the time. What matters is our response. If we see the humanity behind the bones and body bags, if we look in the mirror and realize that we and our families, our children, could just as easily be the victims of genocide, only then can these photos serve the purpose they were meant to serve and finally shove us out of complacency and into action.

IN KIGALI, RWANDA, more than 5,000 prisoners in a former colonial prison wait to be tried for the 1994 genocide in which more than 800,000 Tutsis were slaughtered.

Photograph by Raymond Depardon

OMER BARTOV

Omer Bartov (Israel), John P. Birkelund Distinguished Professor of European History at Brown University, is widely considered one of the world's leading authorities on the Holocaust and genocide. He is the author of six books, including *Germany's War and the Holocaust* (2003), *Mirrors of Destruction: War, Genocide, and Modern Identity* (2000) and *Murder in Our Midst: The Holocaust, Industrial Killing, and Representation* (1996). He also edited *The Holocaust: Origins, Implementation, Aftermath* (2000) and *In God's Name: Genocide and Religion in the Twentieth Century* (2001). Bartov has reviewed books for *The New York Times Book Review* and *The Times Literary Supplement*. He received Guggenheim and National Endowment for the Humanities fellowships as well as Germany's prestigious Humboldt Fellowship. A former member of Harvard's Society of Fellows, Bartov has lectured at Princeton, Harvard, Yale, Oxford, Berkeley and many other universities in Israel, England, France and Germany.

MAGNUM PHOTOS

Magnum Photos, the renowned photographic co-operative owned by its photographer-members, was founded in 1947 by Robert Capa, Henri Cartier-Bresson, George Rodger and David "Chim" Seymour. The Magnum photographers who contributed to this piece— Raymond Depardon, Gilles Peress, Susan Meiselas, Larry Towell, Bruno Barbey, Paolo Pellegrin and Patrick Zachmann—are among the finest photojournalists of their generation. Magnum's participation in *What Matters* was kindly arranged by Michael Shulman, director of publishing and multimedia in Magnum's New York bureau.

Raymond Depardon

THE SCORCHED EARTH OF DARFUR

The Twenty-First Century's First Genocide

THE FIRST GENOCIDE OF THE TWENTY-FIRST CENTURY is under way in Darfur. In fact, it has been under way for five years now as, once again, the world stands by. The human stakes are enormous: 2.5 million Darfurians have been ethnically cleansed from their villages and farms and penned in concentration camps, surrounded by marauding, predatory government-supported Janjaweed militiamen, Darfur's supercharged version of America's Ku Klux Klan.

These agents of genocidal state violence rape women who leave the euphemistically named "internally displaced persons" camps to gather food for their families, and they kill the men and boys. Some 400,000 people have perished so far. All in all, roughly four million people need emergency aid, which the Khartoum regime has repeatedly blocked and manipulated, using food deprivation as yet another form of atrocity.

by **SAMANTHA POWER** *and* **JOHN PRENDERGAST**

photographs by **MARCUS BLEASDALE**

REFUGEES FLEE across the Darfurian desert toward the border with Chad.

The United States and its allies have spent nearly $3 billion in the form of humanitarian assistance to treat the symptoms of mass violence in Darfur, but they have mostly ignored the causes. They pressed for humanitarian access to Darfur without doing what is necessary to help the homeless return to their torched villages and farms. They authorized the deployment of a UN-led peacekeeping mission four years after the crisis erupted, but then lacked the resolve to penalize Sudanese officials who obstructed the deployment of the troops. Indeed, UN member states could not even rally the essential military assets necessary to give the force a fighting chance in a region the size of France. They denounced atrocities and authorized investigations by the International Criminal Court, but then failed to share vital information with the prosecutor, and neither supported nor facilitated the arrest of the war criminals indicted by the court.

In order to ameliorate the human rights and humanitarian emergency and address the roots of the crisis, the United States must work far more robustly and multilaterally to protect the people, promote the peace and punish the perpetrators—the three Ps of genocide prevention.

First and most urgently in such crises, the civilian population must be protected. In September 2005, more than 150 UN member states agreed that they bore the "responsibility to protect" civilians wherever and whenever they are at risk of a massacre. Yet those same countries have failed miserably to uphold this newly codified norm. An effective UN-led protection force in Darfur is not a panacea, but it would help protect thousands of people from further depredations at the hands of militias, government soldiers and rebel forces. Such a force must be large enough to reach the most isolated displaced people and deter abuses, thus encouraging those in the camps to return home so they can rebuild and plant their crops in order to avoid perpetual famine.

Second, the United States must demonstrate much more substantial leadership in promoting a peaceful settlement of Darfur's increasingly complicated conflict. That can work. In January 2005, largely thanks to aggressive US diplomacy, the Sudanese government settled a two-decade-long conflict with rebels in southern

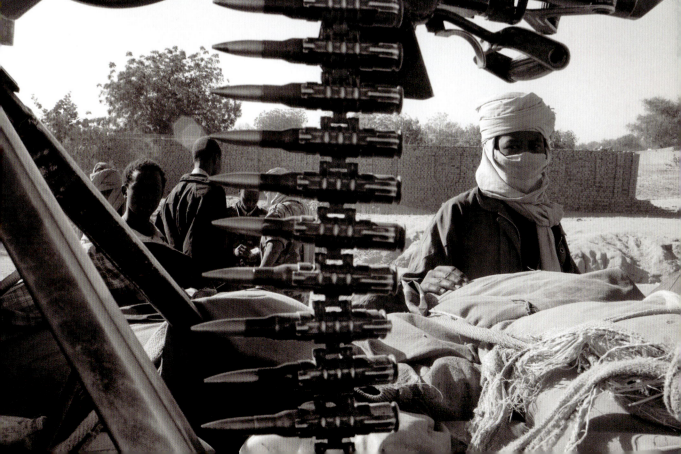

THE REMAINS of a village near the Chad-Darfur border that was attacked by Sudanese rebels. More than forty civilians were killed or injured.

Sudan that had claimed two million lives. Multilateral pressures and incentives—combined with sustained and determined diplomacy—caused Khartoum to cooperate in other instances as well: this same regime expelled Osama bin Laden, abandoned its support for Al Qaeda, halted a resurgent slave trade, ceased aerial bombing in southern Sudan and ended population clearing around its southern oil fields, thus demonstrating that meaningful, sustained pressure and engagement can make all the difference.

At times it has been China and Europe who have left the United States looking unilateral on Sudan. Some European powers seemed to mute their criticisms in the hopes of making commercial investments in Sudan, particularly in the oil industry. China, which has already invested billions in Sudan, protected the Khartoum regime in the UN Security Council, provided weapons to the government and largely remained silent as the genocide unfolded. If

DISPLACED DARFURIANS flee their bombed village to spend the night hidden in the mountains.

UN Secretary-General Ban Ki-moon, with quiet but meaningful American political, financial and logistic backing, were to take the lead in moving the peace process forward and uniting the international community, European and African countries would probably be far more receptive than they would be to Washington alone, which has reduced international legitimacy as a result of the Iraq war. For example, the secretary-general could challenge British prime minister Gordon Brown and French president Nicolas Sarkozy to fulfill their pledge to travel to Darfur to support the peace process, and he could join them in setting a date for the trip and traveling with them. He could also travel to the region and help push for a first draft of an eventual peace proposal, in order to fast-track a negotiations process that has languished for far too long.

The Sudanese regime does indeed take notice when the United States and Europe work together. Most importantly, China's positive

SUDANESE REFUGEES seek shelter from the midday heat and government aircraft under a tree in Disa, northern Darfur.

REFUGEES STRUGGLE to raise their collapsed donkey after a thirty-four-day march toward safety in Chad.

The atrocities in Darfur have given the US government and its citizens their second chance in a generation to stop a genocide.

engagement would be instrumental in shifting Sudanese calculations. Therefore, coordinated US, Chinese and European involvement in support of peace—working closely with the African Union and the United Nations—could pay immediate dividends.

Third, the United States must use all its leverage to turn up the heat and punish the perpetrators in Khartoum. The United States should lead the UN Security Council in imposing multilateral, targeted sanctions—travel bans and asset freezes—against the members of Sudan's regime who are most directly responsible for the atrocities in Darfur and for the obstruction of the deployment of the UN-led protection force. The United States and Europe could also do far more to help accelerate further indictments, by the International Criminal Court, of those officials most culpable for orchestrating genocidal violence and obstructing the UN deployment. It is important to remember that the regime in Khartoum is not the Taliban, and the country's president, Omar al-Bashir, is not Saddam Hussein. Bashir and his henchmen are far more sensitive to world opinion. They do not want to be placed in the international penalty box or isolated for their behavior. But was easy for the regime to withstand unilateral US actions, which for years were viewed as highly partisan and the result of a narrow Bush administration agenda pursued globally against Islamic regimes.

The silver lining in the dark cloud of Darfur's war is the development of a mass movement in the United States, with smaller but equally passionate networks in other countries, dedicated to ending genocide in Darfur and wherever else it might occur. The potential of this permanent constituency to confront atrocities is enormous, because until there is a political cost for inaction in capitals around the world, the same pattern of strong rhetoric and weak action will be played out over and over again.

In the United States, Jewish groups, evangelicals, people moved by the film *Hotel Rwanda* and students teamed up to compel the Bush administration to respond in some way to the civilian suffering in Darfur. On some 500 college campuses, students organized groups to pressure their political representatives to take action on Darfur. Similar groups in some 400 high schools are currently grooming the next generation of citizen activists. Although the Bush administration was consumed with wars in Iraq and Afghanistan, as well as profound strategic challenges in North Korea, Lebanon, Iran and Israel, politically it had no choice but to denounce the atrocities in Darfur as genocide, to keep the displaced-persons camps on US-funded life support and to press for the deployment of the UN protection force, however ineffective.

These measures, which would not have been undertaken without domestic demand from below, saved lives. But they did not save enough lives. The Bush administration did not make stopping genocide a priority, and other countries don't seem to think much about Darfur at all.

The twentieth century was a century of genocide, but also one of remorse. Museums were built across the world to commemorate our regret over doing too little to stop Hitler's extermination of the Jews. An American president, Bill Clinton, traveled all the way to Rwanda to apologize for having done too little to stop the slaughter of 800,000 Rwandans. The atrocities in Darfur have given the US government and its citizens a second chance in a generation to finally bring the country's diplomatic and economic leverage to bear in order to stop genocide. American citizens have seized that chance. If nothing changes, it is their political leaders who will be judged harshly by history. The first genocide of the twenty-first century will have happened on their watch.

A WOMAN RETURNS HOME as night falls. She risks rape by government soldiers and rebels based in the area.

THE DJAMAL HIMEDE refugee camp is home to more than 20,000 people displaced by Janjaweed attacks.

MARCUS BLEASDALE

Marcus Bleasdale (UK), is widely published in periodicals such as *The Sunday Times Magazine, The Telegraph Magazine, The New Yorker, Time, Newsweek* and *National Geographic*. In 2002, *Photo District News* recognized his book about the brutal conflict in the Democratic Republic of the Congo, *One Hundred Years of Darkness*, as one of the year's best. In 2004 he was named UNICEF Photographer of the Year for his work in Darfur.

SAMANTHA POWER

Samantha Power (US) is Anna Lindh Professor of Practice of Global Leadership and Public Policy at Harvard's John F. Kennedy School of Government. She is the author of *Chasing the Flame: Sergio Vieira de Mello and the Fight to Save the World* (Penguin, 2008). Her book *A Problem from Hell: America and the Age of Genocide* won the 2003 Pulitzer Prize for general non-fiction, the National Book Critics Circle Award for general nonfiction, and the Council on Foreign Relations' prize for best book on US foreign policy. Power was founding executive director of the Carr Center for Human Rights Policy (1998-2002). From 1993 to 1996, she covered wars in the former Yugoslavia for *U.S. News and World Report, The Boston Globe*, and *The New Republic*. A graduate of Yale University and Harvard Law School, she is a foreign policy adviser to Barack Obama.

JOHN PRENDERGAST

John Prendergast (US) is cochair of the Enough Project, which works to end genocide in Africa. He was director of African affairs at the National Security Council under President Clinton. Prendergast has also worked for the US State Department, members of Congress, the United Nations, human rights organizations and think tanks. He has authored eight books about Africa, including *Not on Our Watch* (with actor-activist Don Cheadle), a *New York Times* bestseller, and *God, Oil and Country: Changing the Logic of War in Sudan*. Prendergast travels regularly to Africa's war zones on fact-finding missions, peacemaking initiatives and awareness-raising trips. He is a visiting professor at the University of San Diego and the American University in Cairo.

GLOBAL JIHAD
Before and After 9/11

IN THE SECOND HALF OF THE TWENTIETH CENTURY a fierce battle raged in the world of Islam, pitting clusters of self-styled "warriors of God" against pro-Western semi-secular authoritarian regimes. From Iran to Saudi Arabia to Egypt, Algeria and Morocco, warriors of God, or jihadists, launched remorseless attacks against pro-Western regimes in order to establish the rule of sharia, or Qur'anic law.

Since its inception in the early 1970s, contemporary jihadism has been preoccupied with fighting America's client states in the Muslim world. Thus the target of jihadists has long been "al-Adou al-Qareeb," or "the near enemy," the "apostate" Muslim governments in the Middle East and South Asia. Until the mid-1990s, jihadist groups were not interested in attacking the United States directly. Jihadists set their sights on pro-Western regimes in Egypt, Algeria, Pakistan and Saudi Arabia rather than directly confronting "al-Adou al-Baeed," or "the far enemy." Ayman Zawahiri, Al Qaeda's number-two leader, advised his followers as late as 1995 that "the road to Jerusalem goes through Cairo." In other words,

by **FAWAZ A. GERGES**
photographs by **THE ASSOCIATED PRESS**

A MASKED Islamic Jihad militant during a demonstration against an Israeli offensive in Gaza.

Photograph by Muhammed Muheisen

the liberation of Palestine—a primary goal of the jihadist movement—must wait until Islamic governments rule Muslim lands.

During interviews conducted over the last fifteen years, dissident Islamists and jihadists have consistently told me that the most effective way to expel Western influence from Muslim society was to dismantle the oppressive political order that succeeded British and French colonial rule. "Once the local agents of Western imperialism are ousted, America and Europe would no longer dominate our internal affairs," insisted a former associate of Zawahiri. "The Crusaders [America and its allies] exercise control through local proxies."

FIRST TO FALL: THE ISLAMIC REVOLUTION IN IRAN

In 1979, the Shah of Iran—once the head of the most powerful American client state in the region—became the first victim of this titanic struggle when he was overthrown by radical Iranian clerics who followed the teachings of the Ayatollah Khomeini. The radicalized clergy put opposition to America's foreign policy at the

Right:
BOTH TOWERS of the World Trade Center burn behind the Empire State Building after jetliners hijacked by Al Qaeda operatives crashed into both towers.

Far right:
A MAN FALLS headfirst from the north tower of the World Trade Center.

Photographs by Marty Lederhandler and Richard Drew

A MAN WALKS PAST
photos of people missing
after the attacks on the
World Trade Center, pasted
to walls outside the New
York University Medical
Center in lower Manhattan.

Photograph by Ted S. Warren

center of their Islamic revolution. They also tried, with limited success, to export their fierce ideology to neighboring countries.

Shortly after his triumphant return from exile, Khomeini called for the dissolution of sectarian and national walls between Muslim believers. His impassioned rhetoric reverberated throughout the Islamic world. And soon, Shiite communities in the Gulf saw the 1979 Iranian revolution as a prelude to their own uprisings against Sunni-minority regimes in Iraq and Bahrain. Muslims of all stripes began to see Iran's clerical regime as a compelling political alternative to the secular, authoritarian and dismally corrupt regimes in their own countries.

The white-bearded Khomeini made his revolutionary ambitions clear: "We shall export our revolution to the whole world. Until the cry 'there is no God but God' resounds over the whole world, there will be struggle. . . . Islam is the religion of militant individuals who are committed to truth and justice. It is the religion of those who desire freedom and independence. It is the

school of those who struggle against imperialism."

Shiite and Sunni Muslims alike felt renewed and empowered by Khomeini's Islamic revolution. In numerous interviews, militants and activists from both communities told me that they viewed Khomeini's revolution as a strategic model that could be emulated outside of Iran. Indeed, if Khomeini, living in exile, could overthrow the most powerful dictatorship in the Middle East, what could stop similar uprisings in other countries? "[He] taught us a significant lesson," confided an Egyptian Islamic Jihad member. "Political will and charisma could overcome tyranny."

Though many Sunni jihadists are deeply hostile to Shiite doctrine, those I interviewed still said they were inspired by Khomeini's success in Iran. A few months after his takeover, hundreds of armed Saudi fanatics seized the Great Mosque in Mecca, Islam's holiest shrine, exposing the fragility of the oil-rich Saudi monarchy. At approximately the same time, Egyptian president Anwar Sadat signed the 1979 Camp David Accords with Israel,

IN LAHORE, PAKISTAN,
a hawker sells posters celebrating Osama bin Laden during a rally protesting US air strikes on neighboring Afghanistan.

Photograph by K. M. Chaudary

PALESTINIAN GUNMEN
who identify themselves
as members of the Islamic
Jihad shoot a man in a
public square in the West
Bank town of Jenin. The
man, who was executed in
front of hundreds of people,
was accused of giving information to Israeli authorities.

Photograph by Mohammed Ballas

enraging Egyptians, Palestinians and most of the Arab world. Sadat paid with his life for defying the Arab consensus on Israel and ending the state of war with the Jewish state.

"Sadat stabbed us all in the back," said a former jihadist indicted for his role in Sadat's assassination. He told me that Sadat's betrayals were manifold, ranging from harassing religious activists to embracing the "Great Satan" by allying Egypt with the United States. When Sadat and his wife, Jihan, personally offered refuge to the shah after the Iranian revolution in 1979, there was no turning back. He was doomed.

On a sunny morning in October 1981, Sadat, resplendent in a ceremonial uniform, watched a military parade from his reviewing stand. The entire Egyptian political apparatus was assembled and in uniform, celebrating the tenacity of Egyptian forces in the 1973 Arab-Israeli War. With the crowd distracted by an aerial display of fighter jets, a military truck stopped in full view of the television cameras. Four men jumped out, sprayed the reviewing stand with automatic gunfire and threw grenades. In a phrase that would soon be repeated throughout the Muslim world, the ringleader shouted, "I am Khaled al-Islambuli. I have killed Pharaoh and I do not fear death."

PHASE 2: THE AFGHAN WAR

Unlike their Shiite counterparts in Iran, Sunni militants in Saudi Arabia and Egypt failed to seize political power. But they did gain global momentum and an institutionalized organization when thousands of recruits flooded into Afghanistan to repel Soviet communist forces.

The 1979 Soviet invasion of Afghanistan, ten months after the fall of the shah, reminded American officials that their decades-long battle against communism trumped their more recent feud with the radical mullahs of Tehran. As President Jimmy Carter said, the Soviet invasion "could pose the most serious threat to the peace since the Second World War." Therefore, when Russian troops marched into Afghanistan, the United States swiftly mobilized Islamic resistance, tapping anticommunist sentiments among the fundamentalist clergy in Iran and elsewhere.

In a phrase that would soon be repeated throughout the Muslim world, the ringleader shouted, "I am Khaled al-Islambuli. I have killed Pharaoh and I do not fear death."

IN THE WEST BANK'S
Jenin refugee camp, young supporters of Islamic Jihad carry toy guns as they walk next to militants dressed as suicide bombers during a rally to mark the fifth anniversary of the Israeli army's Operation Defensive Shield.

Photograph by Mohammed Ballas

According to Zbigniew Brzezinski, national security adviser to President Carter, containing Soviet communism meant avoiding anything that could split Islamic opposition to the Russians. "It now seemed to me more important to forge an anti-Soviet Islamic coalition," Brzezinski stressed.

The Carter and Reagan administrations both cooperated with Islamists in an effort to harness their ideological fervor as a weapon against communist expansionism. Successive American administrations provided the Afghan mujahideen with billions of dollars and facilitated the flow of foreign jihadists across the porous Pakistani border. When Reagan administration officials decided to turn Afghanistan into Russia's Vietnam and bleed the "evil empire" into bankruptcy, their natural allies were the warriors of God.

Prodded by the United States, Saudi Arabia and Pakistan fully supported the Afghan jihad. The Saudis reasoned that they could outbid Khomeini's revolutionary call by exporting the radical anti-

government fervor of Sunni youth to a faraway land. Saudi Arabian Airlines even created a "jihad price-cut," offering a 75 percent discount to volunteers flying to Afghanistan. Saudi rulers bankrolled the jihad caravan with billions of US oil dollars.

Pakistan, despite its egregiously bad human rights record, has long been America's keystone client state in Central and South Asia. President Mohammed Zia ul-Haq, who led a successful coup d'etat against Prime Minister Zulifaqar Ali Bhutto and then hanged him, turned the struggle against the Soviets in Afghanistan into a holy war that inspired Pakistani zealots. Pakistan became the main transit point for American money, arms, intelligence and training. Other Muslim states, including Egypt, Algeria, Indonesia and Turkey, also provided foot soldiers.

Thus Afghanistan became the rallying point for the first modern transnational army of Islamic warriors: the so-called Afghan Arabs. Not since the height of the Ottoman Empire had so

A GUNMAN from Islamic Jihad stands over the bodies of four Palestinians in a makeshift morgue after they were killed during an Israeli army operation in the Rafah refugee camp, southern Gaza Strip.

Photograph by Khalil Hamra

many Muslims from so many different lands, speaking so many different languages, journeyed to distant battlefields to fight a common foe. These mujahideen were mobile, well trained and ready to confront an enemy anywhere at any time. Their focus quickly became international jihad, not just local jihad.

For a fleeting moment in Afghanistan, in the eyes of all Muslims, there existed a community of believers united in arms against foreign encroachment and aggression. A Yemeni veteran reminisces: "[It] reminded Muslims of all colors and races that what unites us is much more important than the superficial differences wrought by colonialism, secular nationalism and other material ideologies. We felt we were on the verge of reenacting and reliving the Golden Age of our blessed ancestors."

When the Russians finally retreated from Afghanistan in 1989, the mujahideen did not disband and go home. The thousands of Arab volunteers, emboldened by their victory over the Soviet superpower, offered their services as mercenaries in other conflicts. It is a story as old as human history. Those infected with the virus of utopian mission can no longer settle for the mundane. Their victory in Afghanistan fed their taste for adventurism. And their leaders—Ayman Zawahiri, Osama bin Laden and their cohorts—now entertained grand illusions of expelling all American influence from the world of Islam and creating Allah's kingdom on that holy land.

In his memoirs, serialized by the London-based newspaper *Al-Asharq Al-Awsat*, Zawahiri boasts that "the jihad battles in Afghanistan destroyed the myth of a [superpower] in the minds of young Muslim mujahideen. The Soviet Union, a superpower with the largest land army in the world, was destroyed, and the remnants of its troops fled Afghanistan before the eyes of the Muslim youths and with their participation."

Emboldened by their victory, the Afghan Arabs had no interest in returning home, and those who did were hardly welcomed as heroes. Muslim rulers feared that their zealotry and guerrilla warfare experience could destabilize their own regimes. So they disowned the jihadist movement that they had worked so hard to organize a decade earlier. The Afghan War veterans, for their part,

VICTIMS IN BODY BAGS
at the scene of a
suicide bombing of a city
bus in Jerusalem.

Photograph by Oded Balilty

saw themselves as the vanguard of the *ummah* (pan-Arab nation), not as citizens of discredited states imposed by Europe on the ashes of Ottoman glory. The Afghan experience infused the jihadists with hubris. Having forcibly evicted a superpower from Central Asia, they now felt that they could defeat the corrupt, treacherous and ungrateful governments of their home countries.

In the years following the Soviet defeat, hundreds of Afghan War veterans clandestinely waged bloody struggles against local authorities. Throughout the 1990s Egypt and Algeria, in particular, faced fierce jihadist insurgencies that killed more than 100,000 civilians and threatened the very survival of these Western client regimes.

But by the second half of the 1990s, jihadists had been strategically defeated in Egypt, Algeria and elsewhere. Most local jihadists were no match for the security apparatuses of the incumbent regimes, and eventually they declared a unilateral cease-fire—in this case, a euphemism for surrender. Their defeat was caused not only by the brutality of their opponents' intelligence services but by the failure of the jihadists to nurture a viable base of social support. Their over-reliance on violence, coupled with their lack of a political vision, eventually alienated the warriors of God from the mainstream. Forced to choose between the status quo—as corrupt and unpleasant as it was—and fundamentalists jockeying for martyrdom, most Muslims chose neutrality, denying the militants the partisan support they desperately needed.

PHASE 3: THE RISE OF THE GLOBAL JIHAD

As the battle against Muslim tyrants failed, a tiny group of militants led by Osama bin Laden and Ayman Zawahiri launched a campaign to hijack the jihadist movement. They shifted the movement's focus away from Muslim "renegades" and instead targeted the United States and its Western allies, the so-called far enemy. The September 11 attack on US targets was bin Laden's attempt—some would say desperate attempt—to turn political fortune in his favor and prove, in one decisive attack, that he and his brethren were the true vanguard of the *ummah*.

The immediate catalyst for bin Laden's murderous attack was the US military intervention during the 1990 Gulf War and

America's subsequent decision to permanently station US troops in Saudi Arabia, the holy birthplace and homeland of Islam. In Muslim eyes, Saudi Arabia is sacred land—at least as important to Islam as Jerusalem is to Jews.

There were three pivotal factors in bin Laden's decision to target civilians with suicide bombings. First, Ayman Zawahiri, ideologue and theoretician of jihadism, convinced bin Laden that suicide bombing was a legitimate means of warfare; second, bin Laden blamed his 1990s expulsion from Sudan on Saudi Arabia and the United States; and, finally, bin Laden misjudged the mettle of the American people, thinking that killing Americans in their homeland would make them buckle. This opinion may have been nourished by America's failure to respond forcefully to the suicide bombing of the USS *Cole* in October 2000.

AMID BILLOWS OF TEAR GAS, a Palestinian boy throws a stone at Israeli army forces during clashes in Qabatiya village, near the West Bank town of Jenin.

Photograph by Emilio Morenatti

Ironically, bin Laden's September 11 attack did not have widespread support within the jihadist movement. In fact, 9/11 uncovered deep fissures in the movement that soon escalated into open civil war. Leading jihadists have authored books and articles condemning Al Qaeda's terrorist tactics and its deviation from Islamic doctrine. Unfortunately, this "war within," which should have been the most important weapon in America's arsenal against militant Islam, was barely noticed by either US policymakers or the American media.

During interviews conducted over the last decade, many former jihadists told me that while they took delight in America's humiliation at the hands of Al Qaeda, they feared that it would provoke military reprisals that could endanger the survival of the Islamist movement. As a result of this internal dissent, bin Laden and Zawahiri could not provide the steady stream of fresh recruits they promised their fundamentalist base in Afghanistan, and only a trickle of volunteers came to defend the beleaguered Taliban.

COSTS OF THE US "WAR ON TERROR"

To grasp why the jihad went global, it is necessary to understand how larger geopolitical trends have motivated local jihadists. Analyzing jihadists as social actors driven by political, religious and geostrategic concerns would benefit policymakers in the United States and the world at large. Such knowledge would promote more nuanced political and diplomatic approaches to the social phenomenon of the global jihad.

Sadly, the United States has persistently viewed terrorism as ahistorical and apolitical—a moral mutation that can be battered away with military might rather than a social phenomenon that could be addressed more subtly. After 9/11, the dominant narrative in Washington significantly underplayed the role that politics and foreign policy plays in promoting violence and constantly underestimates political means as a way to combat this violence. From 9/11 forward, the Bush administration, while paying lip service to politics and diplomacy, counterproductively waged all-out war against what was initially a weak and fractured foe.

The expansion of the US war on terror radicalized a critical segment of mainstream Muslim opinion. Ordinary Muslims now perceive American foreign policy as antagonistic to their religion and values. Even those who originally opposed bin Laden's strategy are having second thoughts, believing that "he is defending the *ummah*," as one aspiring Arab poet told me. US policymakers do not seem to appreciate how their military adventure in Iraq and their unquestioning support for Israel is militarizing mainstream Muslim opinion and legitimizing radical groups across the Arab world.

I have yet to hear a Friday sermon in a mosque in which believers are not reminded to lend a helping hand to their beleaguered Palestinian and Iraqi counterparts. The ability of Lebanon's Hezbollah, or Party of God, to resist the Israeli military onslaught lent credence to Hamas' proponents. "Hezbollah's victory over the mighty Israeli army has broken the psychological barrier of fear among Muslims," a leading political activist in Yemen told me. "We no longer fear American and Israeli military power. We are armed with faith."

Many ordinary Muslims now perceive American foreign policy as antagonistic to their religion and values.

PAUL DADGE HELPS
injured passenger Davinia
Turrell away from Edgware
Road tube (subway) station
in London following a suicide
bombing by Islamic radicals.

Far right:
RESCUE WORKERS line
up bodies beside a bomb-
damaged passenger train
at Atocha station following
a number of explosions
on trains in Madrid.

Photographs by Jane Mingay
and Denis Doyle

Moreover, the US invasion of Iraq and the subsequent viola-
tions of human rights in American prisons there and in
Guantanamo revived Al Qaeda Central and gave it a new lease on
life. The Iraq war created a new generation of radicals who use terrorism as a rule, not an exception. In fact, the American adventure
in Iraq inspired an unprecedented wave of suicide bombings.
Between the time when the US occupation began in 2003 and
2008, Iraq suffered more than 1,000 suicide attacks, more than
double the number carried out by the Tamil Tigers in Sri Lanka,
Hezbollah in Lebanon, and Hamas in Israel, combined.

The jihadi message resonates wherever there are radicalized
political environments, social and political turmoil, and foreign
occupation. In Iraq, Palestine, Afghanistan and elsewhere, suicide
bombing has become a form of resistance that is politically accept-

ISLAMIC MILITANT Ali Ghufron on the first day of his trial in Denpasar, Bali, Indonesia. Ghufron is the operations chief of Jemaah Islamiyah, the Al Qaeda-linked regional terror group blamed for the 2003 nightclub blasts that killed 202 people, mostly foreign tourists. He was sentenced to death.

Photograph by Divo Additya

able to many Muslims. This may be the jihadists' greatest achievement in the Iraq conflict.

Far from "draining the swamp" of terrorism, as US architects of the Iraqi war proclaimed, the war has produced a new Iraq that exports state-of-the-art bombing techniques, most notably to Afghanistan and Pakistan, where insurgents are copying Iraqi suicide bombings and the improvised explosive devices, or IEDs, that proved so devastating to US forces in Iraq's Sunni Triangle. Afghanistan's former masters, the Taliban, have returned, threatening the survival of the US-backed regime in Kabul.

The Taliban and like-minded Pakistani militants also represent a critical threat to the US-backed dictatorship in Islamabad. Suicide bombings are common occurrences in Pakistan, alarming US officials, who put all their eggs in General Musharraf's basket. A case in point was the December 2007 assassination of Pakistani opposition leader Benazir Bhutto, whose death stoked new chaos across the nuclear-armed nation.

The old Iraq, though a place of stunning brutality and repression, never knew suicide terrorism and generally shunned Al Qaeda's ideology and tactics. But since 2006, I have interviewed scores of Arab and Muslim teens all over the Middle East and Europe who say they want to join the fight against the American "occupiers." Many youngsters tell me that they are deeply affected by what they see as external aggression against their religion. They say their local clerics tell them stories about atrocities committed by US soldiers and instruct them that jihad is an individual obligation.

These teenagers—whom I met in the Gulf states, Lebanon, Palestinian refugee camps, Egypt, Jordan, Syria, Spain, France and Italy—are each trying to raise several hundred dollars to make their way to Iraq through Syria. Most have no previous connection to Islamist militancy or Al Qaeda, but now many talk about sacrificing themselves in "martyrdom operations." Based on my interviews with young Muslims, I would argue that if it were not for the logistical and financial impediments, the flow of volunteers from the lands of Islam and Europe into Iraq would exceed the flow of "Afghan Arabs" into Afghanistan in the 1980s. A significant proportion of Islam now views the American invasion of Iraq in the same light as the Soviet invasion of Afghanistan in 1979.

European and US intelligence communities now believe that the war in Iraq helped Al Qaeda Central to revitalize and rebuild its command-and-control infrastructure in the Pakistan-Afghan tribal area. Equally important, Al Qaeda's ideology has now migrated into disfranchised Muslim communities worldwide. America's imperial endeavor in Iraq gave transnational jihadists such as Al Qaeda a new lease on life and new opportunities to make inroads, if not into mainstream Arab hearts and minds, then into a large pool of outraged Muslims in the Middle East and disaffected young European-born Muslims, who now want to resist what they perceive as a Western onslaught on their co-religionists.

Most of the teenagers have no previous connection to Islamist militancy or Al Qaeda, but now they talk about sacrificing themselves in "martyrdom operations."

MICHAEL BERG, *left,*
collapses to the ground in
front of the family home in
West Chester, Pennsylvania,
after learning from the
US State Department that
his son's decapitated body
was found near a highway
in Baghdad.

Photograph by Jacqueline Larma

WHAT CAN BE DONE?

One of the major findings in my two most recent books, *The Far
Enemy: Why Jihad Went Global* and *Journey of the Jihadist: Inside Muslim
Militancy*, is that contrary to conventional wisdom, the dominant
response to Al Qaeda in the Muslim world was initially very hostile,
and few activists, let alone ordinary Muslims, embraced its global
jihad. Before the US invasion of Iraq, Al Qaeda faced a two-front
war, internally and externally, with the interior front, Muslim hostil-
ity to its methods, threatening its very existence. At the outset, bin
Laden and his transnationalist cohorts lost the war of ideas, the struggle for Muslim minds—a critical point largely overlooked by
American commentators and policymakers, who failed to notice the
fault lines separating Al Qaeda from other jihadists and the overwhelming opposition to global jihad within Muslim society at large.

Had the U.S administration and media noticed these internal struggles, they would have had second thoughts about the military expansion of the "war on terror." They would have realized that Al Qaeda was a tiny fringe organization with no viable entrenched constituency. Had they observed the words and deeds of former jihadists and Islamists, they would have known that the jihadist movement was in tatters and that Al Qaeda neither spoke for Islam nor represented religious activists or Muslim public opinion; American commentators and policymakers would also have realized that the internal defeat of Al Qaeda on its home front was, and continues to be, the most effective way to destroy it.

The United States and the international community should have found ways to nourish and support the Muslim forces that inherently opposed the bin Laden network. The path to victory

AN IRAQI MAN mourns over the body of his relative, killed in a suicide bomber attack, in Najaf, 160 kilometers south of Baghdad.

Photo by Alaa Al-Marjani

was not to declare worldwide war against a nonconventional foe with almost no social support while simultaneously settling scores with old regional dictators. That is exactly what bin Laden and his senior associates hoped the United States would do. As Seif al-Adal, Al Qaeda's overall military commander put it in 2005, "The Americans took the bait and fell into our trap."

How should the US have responded to the 9/11 attacks? First, the Bush administration, after toppling the Taliban and pursuing Al Qaeda, should have developed a political vision that sought to resolve the region's simmering conflicts, particularly the Arab-Israeli dispute. Instead, Bush's neocon ideologues unconditionally supported former Israeli prime minister Ariel Sharon and called his war with the Palestinians an extension of the US war on terror. This misguided policy gave radical Hamas credibility in the eyes of the Palestinians and a public mandate to govern.

Second, the Bush administration should have built alliances with Muslim civil societies—particularly mainstream Islamic activists who oppose violence—and kept some distance from corrupt, oppressive local regimes. Instead, ratcheting up the rhetoric, President Bush grouped all Islamists together under the phrase *Islamo-fascists* and told Americans to prepare for a long global struggle. If Washington had better understood the internal political and ideological dynamics of the Muslim world, it would never have militarized the war on terror and played into Al Qaeda's hands.

Third, the Bush administration should have developed a Marshall Plan, with European and Asian partners, to rejuvenate stagnant Middle Eastern economies and institutions. Imagine if the American foreign-policy elite, instead of allocating $500 billion to the Iraq war, had allocated a fraction of that amount to building democratic institutions and civil societies in the Muslim world, healing historic wounds.

Finally, imagine if the Bush administration had genuinely made the democratic paradigm the foundation of its foreign policy toward Muslim societies, using carrots and sticks rather than guns and bombs to persuade dictators to open political systems. The rhetoric of democracy is hollow unless it is translated into concrete actions such as institution-building, reducing huge socioeco-

THREE HOSTAGES—one British, two American—are depicted on an Islamic militant Web site in Iraq.

nomic inequities, resolving regional conflicts and showing a universal commitment to human rights and the rule of law.

The next administration must begin the process of extracting US forces from Iraq's shifting sands and resolving the region's simmering conflicts, particularly the shedding of Jewish and Palestinian blood. The major foreign-policy challenge will be facing the complexity of the region's troubles—and crafting a grand strategy not only for Iraq but for the region as a whole. This grand strategy—based on the realities of the region, not the so-called war on terror—will be the most effective means of defeating the global jihad.

THE CENTRAL CELLBLOCK
passage at Camp Delta
2 and 3 maximum-security
detention center, at the US
naval base in Guantanamo
Bay, Cuba, where alleged
Islamic combatants and
terrorists are held captive.

Photograph by Brennan Linsley

FAWAZ A. GERGES

Fawaz A. Gerges (US / b. Lebanon) holds the Christian A. Johnson Chair in Muslim Politics and International Affairs at Sarah Lawrence College. He authored *Journey of the Jihadist: Inside Muslim Militancy* and *The Far Enemy: Why Jihad Went Global*, which was selected by *The Washington Post* as one of the best books in the field. Gerges has taught at Oxford, Harvard and Columbia, and was a research scholar at Princeton. His articles have appeared in *The New York Times, The Washington Post, The Los Angeles Times, The Christian Science Monitor, the International Herald Tribune* and *The Independent* (London). He is regularly interviewed by news sources worldwide, including ABC, CNN, BBC, PBS, CBS, NPR, CBC and Al Jazeera. Gerges has received MacArthur, Fulbright and Carnegie fellowships.

THE ASSOCIATED PRESS

The global jihad takes place on many fronts, and virtually every one is covered daily by AP, the largest group of working photojournalists in the world and the winner of thirty Pulitzer Prizes. This selection of AP photos was compiled and edited by J. David Ake, AP's assistant chief of bureau for photos in Washington, DC, and Michael Feldman, international photo editor, in New York.

AN IRAQI SOLDIER shouts while showing family pictures retrieved from a minibus blown up by a suicide bomber in Baghdad.

Photograph by Khalid Mohammed

BITTER FRUIT

Behind the Scenes, America Buries Its Iraq War Dead

WAR IS NOTHING UNTIL YOU SEE IT. Iraq is barely real, just something that keeps happening to other people very far away. Only stark, clear, undeniable images can make us realize what's happening.

But there are only a few images out there. Photographs of the war's horrible reality—the corpses, the mangled bodies, the dreadfully wounded victims—rarely appear in the US media. The war is largely invisible.

That's the way our government likes it. The administration and its allies have tried to keep the Iraq war out of sight. The Bush White House banned photographs of the coffins of US soldiers being shipped home, and President Bush wouldn't attend the funerals of troops killed in Iraq. In 2004, when the ABC news program *Nightline* ran photographs of the faces of every American soldier killed in Iraq, conservative groups were outraged and accused the show of pursuing an anti-war agenda and damaging troop morale.

Of course, there's nothing unusual about this. The men who make war never want these images shown. In World War II, the Roosevelt administration forbade the media from publishing

ELLSWORTH, WISCONSIN: Funeral service for Private First Class Bert Hoyer, who was killed in Iraq.

by **GARY KAMIYA**
photographs by **PAUL FUSCO**

Once a war starts, the corpses magically disappear. Death is too powerful and chaotic a force to be let loose when national unity must be preserved.

photographs of dead GIs until 1943, when *Life* magazine ran a photo showing dead US Marines sprawled facedown on a beach in New Guinea. The media became bolder in Vietnam, but that only taught officials how important it is to control the images seen on the home front: film of US troops coming home in body bags helped turn Americans against the war.

War is about killing people, and if you're going to really cover war, you have to show death—everything else is an evasion. You wouldn't think this would be a problem. After all, Americans love images of violence. Our culture is juiced by death, and the bloodier the images, the bigger the thrill. Hollywood floats to the bank on a sea of blood. Bodies splatter ever more realistically in slasher movies and video games. The bloated bodies in old photographs of the Civil War fascinate us. We can't get enough of death—so long as it's fictional or at a safe historical distance.

But once a war starts, the corpses magically disappear. For death is too powerful and chaotic a force to be let loose when national unity must be preserved and national myths upheld. Officials know that the unspeakable truth about war erodes public support. Blood is a powerful solvent; it dissolves empty patriotism and lofty lies. Rotting bodies and mutilated children ruin the flag-waving narrative. And the old cliché is true: images of war are far more potent than words. Nick Ut's photograph of a nine-year-old Vietnamese girl running down a road, screaming in pain from the napalm burning her back, brought the horror of Vietnam home in a way that even the best print reporting could not. A piece of writing can be majestic, but a great photograph is unfathomable. And war is unfathomable.

But the party most responsible for keeping the Iraq war invisible isn't the administration: it's the media. The media has the power to show Americans shocking images of the war, and it has mostly decided not to do that. This isn't surprising; it's the default position, and there's no incentive to change it. So-called graphic pictures cause advertisers to cancel, offend readers and draw accusations of lack of patriotism or even treason. Taste issues, business concerns and fear of controversy far outweigh some free-floating, idealistic desire to tell the whole truth.

We like to pretend that the media is an independent force, one that operates outside the constraints imposed by state and society. But that's a myth. As the US media's disgraceful performance during the run-up to Iraq showed, at times of war or national crisis, the media tends to revert to a quasi-official role. The media failed after 9/11 because it decided that reflecting some imagined national consensus was more important than aggressively questioning the Bush administration's rationale for starting the Iraq war. And the same deference to convention has informed its coverage of that war. As big media organizations become increasingly indistinguishable from other corporations—docile, centrist and risk-averse—they are less and less willing to challenge taboos.

In fact, the media has covered Iraq pretty much by the book. Its coverage hasn't been any better or worse than its coverage of other wars. There's a kind of unwritten code that governs news decisions, and the semi-guerrilla nature of the Iraq war, along with the fact that a baseline of coverage has already been established, makes it very hard for editors to justify increased exposure. This war is endless; it lacks defining moments, it has no large battles and there are comparatively few American casualties. All these factors keep it off the front page.

Besides, there's no audience. Few people are fully engaged with the Iraq war anymore. Even those opposed to it, who make up a majority of the country, seem to have grown exhausted or disillusioned or bored. And, crucially, because there's no draft, the war doesn't personally touch most Americans. Protests, elections, writing letters to Congress—none have had any effect. Pointless, endless, accompanied by a faint drip-drip of US casualties, Iraq runs on autopilot. As the war drones on, dropping from page one to page six to page sixteen, fading from the evening TV news shows, a kind of vicious cycle of apathy is created. Because there's no "news"—that is, nothing significantly different from yesterday's horrors—the media ignores the war. And because the media ignores the war, the public forgets about the war, and because the public forgets about the war, the media ignores the war. As the 2008 election campaign got under way, CNN polls showed the Iraq war falling well below the economy on the electorate's list of top concerns. If Iraq goes on

Following pages, clockwise from top left:
FUNERAL SERVICES for Private Bryan Nicholas "Nick" Spry in Chestertown, Maryland; Specialist Bruce Miller in East Orange, New Jersey; Private First Class Bert Hoyer in Ellsworth, Wisconsin; and Sergeant Anthony Lagman in Yonkers, New York. All were killed in Iraq.

If the Iraq war goes on long enough, it may be the first war in history to be forgotten by everyone except those who are actually fighting and the families of those who are dying.

long enough, it may be the first war in history to be completely forgotten by everyone except those who are actually fighting and the families of those who are dying.

This is all normal. We're all secretly relieved not to have to think about the war. Life goes on. We move on. But we leave something behind, something having to do with being a citizen, and a human being.

When a country starts a war, its citizens need to know what the consequences are. That's why we need war reporting. No matter

how normal and reassuring it is to ignore the horrible things that happen in war, it's wrong. Because if we don't know what war really is, we'll be tempted to launch wars without good reason. And if we don't accept responsibility for the consequences of wars waged in our name, we don't deserve to be called citizens.

Which is why Paul Fusco's photographs of the funerals of American soldiers killed in Iraq are so terribly necessary. Fusco's photographs are a painful reminder of the terrible cost of war, a cost borne not just by the dead and wounded and mentally scarred

HAVERSTRAW, NEW YORK: Funeral service for US Army Specialist Manuel "Manny" Lopez III, who was killed in Iraq when his vehicle was hit by a rocket-propelled grenade.

soldiers who fight, but by their families and loved ones. As you look at these pictures, at the anguished faces of mothers and fathers, wives and brothers and children, the grand words on war monuments disappear, and you're left with a simple question: How would you feel if the person you loved most in the world was taken from you?

For that is what it comes down to, when the headlines and speeches are done. It comes down to a big box covered in a flag containing what used to be a person, and a bunch of people just like you and me standing around with a huge hole punched through their lives.

These faces make us weep. But they should also make us think. One thing they should make us think about is the Iraqis. Take all the heartbreak in Fusco's photographs and multiply it exponentially, and you wouldn't touch what the war has done to the Iraqi people. Hundreds of thousands of Iraqis have died; hundreds of thousands more have been wounded; and millions have been forced into exile. The US invasion triggered one of the greatest human rights calamities in modern history. That *is* a story. But as if taking its lead from the Bush administration, which refuses to keep any records of Iraqi civilian casualties, the American media has barely reported it. They aren't our people, so it isn't our problem.

The war is invisible to most of us. But it isn't invisible to the Americans in Fusco's photographs, or to millions of Iraqis. We owe it to them, as fellow citizens and human beings, to look unflinchingly at the truth, painful as it is. And we owe it to ourselves to remember what war is, so that we do not go lightly into its great darkness.

The war is invisible to most of us. But it isn't invisible to the Americans in Fusco's photographs, or to millions of Iraqis.

BRIDGEPORT, CONNECTICUT: Funeral service for Specialist Tyanna Avery Felder, who was killed in Iraq.

We owe it to ourselves to remember what war is, so that we do not go lightly into its great darkness.

SPRINGFIELD, VERMONT:
Funeral service for Sergeant Scott Rose, who was killed in Iraq. The honor guard is from the local Veterans of Foreign Wars (VFW) posts in Ludlow and Chester.

PAUL FUSCO

As a staff photographer for *LOOK* magazine, Paul Fusco (US) accompanied Robert F. Kennedy's funeral train from New York to Washington, DC. A member of Magnum Photos since 1973, Fusco creates work that deals with social issues worldwide, including essays on the reform of migrant labor practices, coal miners in Appalachia, people living with AIDS and residents of the Mexican state of Chiapas, as well as an ongoing project on children suffering from Chernobyl radiation.

GARY KAMIYA

Gary Kamiya (US) is a cofounder, former executive editor and current writer-at-large at Salon.com. After winning the top undergraduate award in English literature at the University of California, Berkeley, which led to a career as a starving theater critic, he worked at *The San Francisco Examiner*, where he was variously a senior editor at the paper's magazine, book editor, movie critic and media columnist. At Salon, he has reported from the Middle East, covered three Olympics and written about culture, politics, the Israeli-Palestinian crisis and race relations. His work has appeared in *Sports Illustrated, Artforum* and many other magazines, and he is a regular contributor to *The New York Times Book Review*. His essay on Ronald Reagan will appear in the forthcoming *New Literary History of America*.

CHESTERTOWN, MARYLAND: Funeral service for Private Bryan Nicholas Spry, who was killed in Iraq.

THE BOTTOM BILLION

How We Can End Global Poverty

HOMELESS,
Jakarta,
Indonesia.

IT IS MIDMORNING IN MALAWI when we arrive at a small village, Nthandire, about an hour from the capital. We have come over dirt roads, passing women and children walking barefoot with water jugs, wood for fuel, and other bundles. The midmorning temperature is sweltering. In this subsistence maize-growing region of a poor, landlocked country in southern Africa, families cling to life on an unforgiving terrain. This year has been more difficult than usual because the rains have failed, and we see crops withering in the fields.

If the village were filled with able-bodied men who could build rainwater-collecting units on rooftops and in the fields, the situation would not be so dire. But as we arrive in the village, we see no able-bodied young men at all. Older women and dozens of children greet us, but there is not a young man or woman in sight. Where, we ask, are the workers? Out in the fields? The aid worker who led us to the village shakes his head sadly and says no. Nearly all are dead; AIDS has devastated the village.

by **JEFFREY D. SACHS**
photographs by **JAMES NACHTWEY**

It is no good to lecture the dying that they should have done better.

In Nthandire, death's presence has been overwhelming. The grandmothers we meet care for orphaned grandchildren. The margin of survival is extraordinarily narrow; sometimes it closes entirely. One woman has 15 orphaned grandchildren. Her small farm plot, about an acre, is too small to feed her family even when rains are plentiful. Soil nutrients have been so depleted in this part of Malawi that crop yields are only one-third of normal. Because of the drought, she will get almost nothing. She reaches into her apron and pulls out a handful of semi-rotten, bug-infested millet seeds for the gruel she will prepare for dinner—the one meal the children will get that day.

I ask her about the children's health. She points to a girl of about four and says that she contracted malaria last week. The woman carried her grandchild six miles on her back to the local hospital. When they arrived, there was no antimalarial medicine available. They were told to return the next day. When they returned after another twelve-mile round-trip, quinine had miraculously arrived. The child survived, but between one and three million African children die from malaria each year.

As we proceed through the village, I stoop to ask one of the young girls her name and age. She looks seven or eight, but is actually 12, stunted from years of undernutrition. When I ask about her dreams, she says she wants to be a teacher and that she will try hard to achieve that. I know her chances of ever going to secondary school or teachers college are slim.

The plight of Malawi in 2004 was rightly described by Carol Bellamy, former head of UNICEF, as a perfect storm of human deprivation—climatic disaster, poverty, AIDS, malaria, schistosomiasis and other diseases. Facing this horrific maelstrom, the world community displayed a fair bit of hand wringing and even some high-minded rhetoric, but precious little action. It is no good to lecture the dying that they should have done better. It is our task to help them onto the ladder of development, to give them at least a foothold on the bottom rung, then they can climb on their own.

This is a story about ending poverty in our time. It is not a forecast. I am not predicting what will happen, only explaining that it can happen. Currently, more than eight million people around the world die each year simply because they are too poor to stay alive. If

so inclined, our newspapers could accurately report every morning, "More than 20,000 people perished yesterday of extreme poverty." How? The poor die in hospital wards that lack drugs, in villages that lack antimalarial bed nets, in houses that lack safe drinking water. They die namelessly, without public comment.

Since 9/11, the U.S. has waged a war on terrorism, but neglected the deeper causes of global instability. The $500 billion the US spends each year on the military will never buy lasting peace when we spend one-thirtieth of that, around $16 billion, to address the plight of the world's poorest citizens, whose societies are destabilized by extreme poverty. The share of US income devoted to helping the poor has declined for decades—a tiny fraction of what the US has repeatedly promised, and repeatedly failed, to give.

Yet our generation can choose to end extreme poverty by the year 2025. To do it, we must adopt a new method, which I call "clinical economics," to underscore the similarities between good development economics and good clinical medicine. In the past

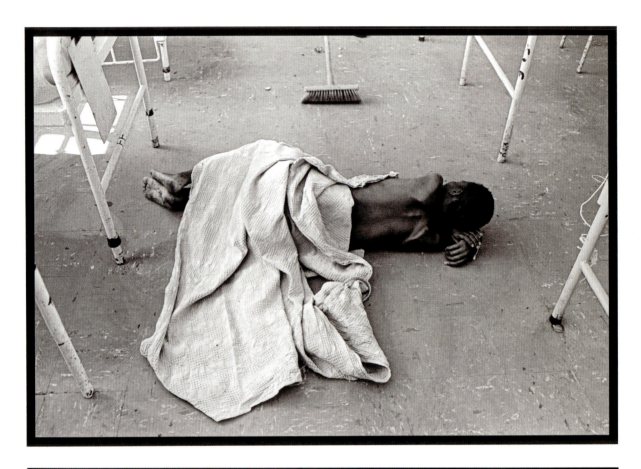

quarter-century, the development economics imposed by rich countries on the poorest countries has been like eighteenth century medicine when doctors used leeches to draw blood, often killing their patients in the process. Development economics needs to be much more like modern medicine: rigorous, insightful and practical. The sources of poverty are multidimensional, and so are the solutions. In my view, clean water, productive soils and functioning health-care systems are as relevant as foreign exchange rates. The task of ending extreme poverty is collective. The end of poverty will require global cooperation among people who have never met and who do not necessarily trust one another.

One part of the puzzle is relatively easy. Most people, with little prodding, would accept the fact that schools, clinics, roads, electricity, ports, soil nutrients, clean water and sanitation are basic necessities, not only for dignity and health, but also to make an economy work. They would also agree that the poor might need help to meet their basic needs. But they might be skeptical that the world could effectively give that help. If, as many think, the poor are poor because they are lazy or their governments are corrupt, how could global cooperation help?

Fortunately, these are misconceptions—only a small fraction of the explanation of why the poor are poor. In all corners of the world, the poor face structural impediments that keep them from reaching even the first rung on the development ladder. Most societies with the right ingredients—good harbors, close contacts with the rich world, favorable climates, adequate energy sources and freedom from endemic disease—have escaped extreme poverty. Our challenge is not mainly to overcome laziness and corruption, but rather to address the solvable problems of geographic isolation, disease and natural hazards, and to do so with new arrangements of political responsibility that can get the job done. We need plans, systems, mutual accountability and financing mechanisms. But even before we put that apparatus in place—what I call economic plumbing—we must understand what such a strategy would mean to the people who can be helped.

Nearly half of the earth's six billion people are poor. As a matter of definition, there are three degrees of poverty: extreme (or absolute) poverty, moderate poverty and relative poverty. Extreme

More than 8 million people around the world die each year simply because they are too poor to stay alive.

Top:
AN OVERCROWDED tuberculosis ward in Harare, Zimbabwe.

Bottom:
HOMELESS CHILDREN, many of them AIDS orphans, sleep on the street in Harare, Zimbabwe.

A WOMAN TAKEN to an emergency feeding center in Somalia established by the Irish charity CONCERN waits for food and medical attention.

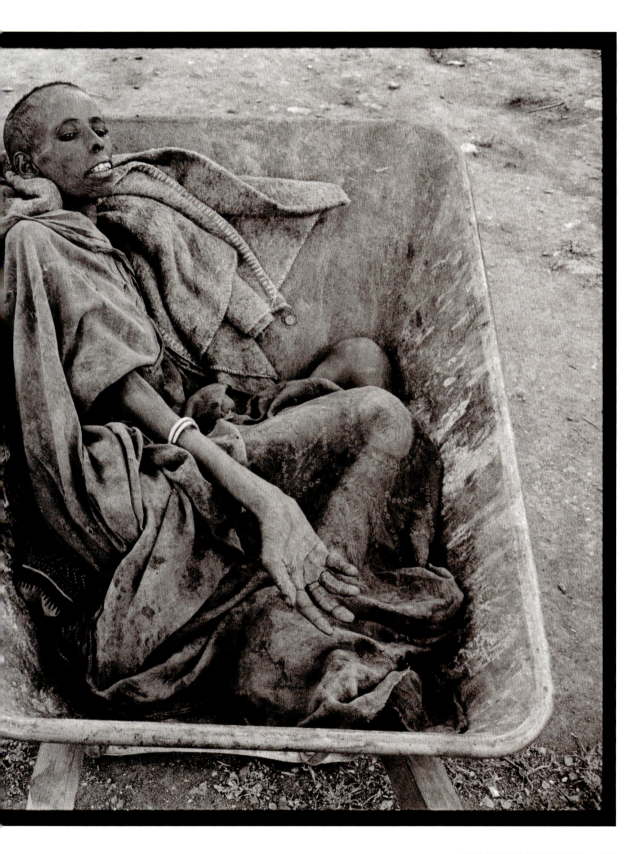

poverty, defined by the World Bank as an income of less than one dollar a day, means that households cannot meet basic survival needs. They are chronically hungry and lack health care, safe drinking water and sanitation. They cannot afford to educate their children and sometimes lack rudimentary shelter and basic articles of clothing, like shoes. This is "the poverty that kills." Extreme poverty now exists only in developing countries. Moderate poverty, defined as living on $1 to $2 a day, refers to conditions in which basic needs are just barely met. Relative poverty, defined by household income below a given proportion of the national average, means lacking things that the middle class takes for granted.

The World Bank estimates that 1.1 billion people live in extreme poverty, down from 1.5 billion in 1981. While that represents significant progress, much of the one-sixth of humanity in extreme poverty suffers the ravages of AIDS, drought, isolation and civil wars, and is thereby trapped in a vicious cycle of deprivation and death. Moreover, while the economic boom in East Asia has helped reduce the proportion of extremely poor in that region from 58 percent in 1981 to 15 percent in 2001, and in South Asia from 52 percent to 31 percent, the situation is more deeply entrenched in Africa, where nearly half of the continent's population lives in extreme poverty—a proportion that has actually risen over the past two decades.

A few centuries ago, vast divides in wealth and poverty did not exist. Nearly everybody was poor, except a tiny minority of rulers and large landowners. Life was just as difficult in much of Europe as it was in India or China. Your great-great-grandparents were, with few exceptions, poor and living on a farm. The onset of the Industrial Revolution, supported by a rise in agricultural productivity, unleashed a period of explosive economic growth. Population and per-capita income rose at rates never before imagined. The global population grew six-fold in just two centuries, while the world's average per-capita income rose even faster—nine-fold between 1820 and 2000. In rich countries, economic growth was even more astounding. In the US, per-capita income increased twenty-five-fold during this period.

In the face of that success, many embraced faulty social theories. When a society is economically dominant, it is easy for its members to assume that their dominance reflects a deeper superiority

—religious, racial, genetic, ethnic, cultural or institutional—rather than an accident of timing or geography.

Such theories justified brutal forms of exploitation during colonial rule, and they persist today among those who don't understand what happened and is still happening in the Third World. The failure of the Third World to grow as rapidly as the First World is the result of a complex mix of factors: geographical, historical and political. Imperial rule often left conquered regions bereft of education, health care, indigenous political leadership and infrastructure. Often, newly independent countries in the post–World War II period made disastrous political and economic choices. But the regions left furthest behind also faced special obstacles: diseases such as malaria, drought-prone climates, extreme isolation in mountains and landlocked regions, the absence of energy resources and other liabilities that locked these areas outside the mainstream of global economic growth. Countries ranging from Bolivia to Malawi to Afghanistan face challenges almost unknown in the rich world, challenges that are at first harrowing to contemplate, but on second thought encouraging in the sense that they lend themselves to practical solutions.

In the past quarter-century, when poor countries have begged the rich world for help, they have been sent to the world money doctor, the International Monetary Fund. Until very recently, the main IMF prescription has been budgetary belt-tightening for patients much too poor to even own belts. IMF-led austerity has frequently resulted in riots, coups and the collapse of public services. Finally, however, that approach has changed.

It took me 20 years to understand what good development economics should be, and I am still learning. In 2004, as director of the UN Millennium Project—which hopes to cut the world's extreme poverty in half by 2015—I spent several eye-opening days with colleagues in a group of eight Kenyan villages known as the Sauri sublocation in the Siaya district of Nyanza province. We visited farms, clinics, hospitals and schools, and found a region beset by hunger, AIDS and malaria. The situation was grim, but salvageable. More than 200 members of the community met with us one afternoon. Hungry, thin and ill, they stayed for three and one-half hours, speaking about their predicament with dignity, eloquence and clarity. They were impoverished, but capable and resourceful. Though

When a society is economically dominant, it is easy for its members to assume that their dominance reflects a deeper superiority rather than an accident of timing or geography.

S pin as we might about American generosity, the poor countries are fully aware of our broken promises.

struggling to survive, they were not dispirited. They were determined to improve their situation, and they knew how to do that.

The meeting took place outside the Bar Sauri Primary School, where headmistress Anne Marcelline Omolo shepherded hundreds of schoolchildren through the travails of daily life. Despite disease, orphanhood and hunger, all thirty-three of the previous year's eighth-grade class had passed the Kenyan national secondary-school exams. We saw why. On their "day off" from school, the eighth-graders sat at their desks from 6:30 a.m. until 6 p.m. studying months in advance for the national examinations. Unfortunately, many who passed the exams would not attend secondary school because they did not have enough money for tuition, uniforms and supplies. Nonetheless, the community supported the eighth-graders during their critical examination year, by providing them with a midday meal, cooked with wood and water the students brought from home. But the community could not afford midday meals for younger children.

When our village meeting got under way, I canvassed the group. Only two of the 200 farmers at the meeting used fertilizer. Around 25 percent used improved fallows with nitrogen-fixing trees, a scientific farming approach in which villagers grow trees that naturally return nitrogen to the soil, dramatically improving yields. The new method could have been used throughout the village had more money been available for trees. The rest of the community farmed tiny plots, sometimes no more than one-quarter acre, with soil so depleted that even when the rains were good, households went hungry. When the rains failed, these households faced death. The real shocker came with my follow-up question. How many farmers had used fertilizers in the past? Every hand in the room shot up. Farmer after farmer described how the fertilizer became too expensive.

As the afternoon unfolded, the gravity of the community's predicament became more apparent. I asked how many households had one or more children orphaned by the AIDS pandemic. Virtually every hand in the room shot up. I asked how many households received remittances from family members living in Nairobi and other cities. They said that only coffins and orphans came back from the cities. I asked how many households suffered from malaria. Three-fourths. How many used antimalarial bed nets? Two out of

200. How many knew about bed nets? All hands up. And how many would like to use bed nets? All hands remained up. The problem, many women explained, is that they cannot afford the bed nets (which sell for a few dollars) even when partially subsidized by international donor agencies.

Once Sauri's residents cooked with locally collected wood. But the number of trees declined, forcing villagers to buy seven pieces of fuel wood in Yala or Muhanda for 30 cents. Not only are seven sticks barely enough to cook one meal, but the lack of 30 cents meant that many villagers had reverted to cooking with cow dung or eating uncooked meals. The dying village's isolation was stunning. There were no cars or trucks, and only a handful of villagers reported that they had ridden in motorized transport during the past year. Around half of the individuals at the meeting said that they had never made a phone call.

My colleagues and I felt that this village—and villages like it—could be rescued, but not without help. Survival depended on

AN UNTOUCHABLE in New Delhi, India, scavenges in a waste dump among vultures.

If, as many think, the poor are poor because they are lazy or their governments are corrupt, how could global cooperation help?

addressing a series of five specific challenges with known, proven, reliable and appropriate technologies and interventions:

1. **AGRICULTURE** With fertilizers, cover crops, irrigation and improved seeds, we knew that Sauri's farmers could triple their food yields and quickly end chronic hunger. Grain could be protected in locally made storage bins using leaves with insecticidal properties from the improved fallow species, tephrosia.

2. **BASIC HEALTH:** A village clinic with one doctor and nurse for 5,000 residents could provide free antimalarial bed nets, effective antimalarial medicines and treatments for HIV/AIDS-related opportunistic infections.

3. **EDUCATION:** Meals for every child at the primary school could improve the kids' health, attendance and the quality of education. Expanded vocational training could teach students modern farming, computer literacy, basic infrastructure maintenance and carpentry.

4. **POWER:** Electricity could be made available with either a power line or an off-grid diesel generator. The electricity could power lights, a computer for the school, pumps for safe well water, machines for milling grain and refrigeration. Students wanted to study after sunset but could not do so without electric lights.

5. **CLEAN WATER AND SANITATION:** With enough water points and latrines, women and children could save countless hours of toil each day fetching water. The water could be provided through a combination of protected springs, rainwater harvesting and other basic technologies.

Ironically, the cost of these services for Sauri's 5,000 residents was only about $70 per person per year. And the benefits were astounding. We knew from the outset that these investments would repay themselves not only in lives saved, children educated and communities preserved, but also in direct commercial returns and self-sustaining economic growth. The results justified our expectation, and as of 2008, there were 79 Millennial Villages in Ethiopia, Ghana, Kenya, Madagascar, Malawi, Mali, Mozambique, Nigeria, Rwanda, Senegal, Tanzania and Uganda. These villages, in turn, are exporting their successful interventions to neighboring villages, and the result is transforming Africa. The international donor community should be thinking round-the-clock about one question: How can the Big Five interventions be applied worldwide?

The outside world has pat answers for extremely impoverished countries, particularly in Africa. Everything comes back to corruption and misrule. Western officials argue that Africa simply needs to behave itself better, to allow market forces to operate without interference by corrupt rulers. Yet the critics of African governance have it wrong. The claim that Africa's corruption is the basic source of its prolonged economic crisis can't withstand serious scrutiny. For fifteen years, I have witnessed how relatively well-governed countries in Africa, such as Ghana, Malawi, Mali and Senegal, failed to prosper, whereas societies in Asia perceived as extensively corrupt, such as Bangladesh, Indonesia and Pakistan, enjoyed rapid economic growth.

What is the explanation? Every example of extreme poverty around the world has some unique bases that need to be diagnosed just as a doctor would diagnose a patient. Africa, for example, is burdened with malaria like no other part of the world, simply because it provides perfect conditions for that disease.

Another myth is that the developed world already gives plenty of aid to the world's poor. Former US Treasury Secretary Paul O'Neill expressed a common frustration when he remarked about aid for Africa: "We've spent trillions of dollars on these problems and we have damn near nothing to show for it." O'Neill was no foe of foreign aid. He wanted to fix the system so that more US aid could

A HOMELESS MAN who lives in the scaffolding beneath a bridge in Jakarta, Indonesia, washes his clothes by a sewer pipe.

be justified. But he was wrong to believe that vast flows of aid to Africa were squandered. President Bush said in a press conference in April 2004 that as "the greatest power on the face of the earth, we have an obligation to help the spread of freedom. We have an obligation to feed the hungry." But how has the US met that obligation?

In recent years, US aid to help farmers in poor countries has been around $200 million per year, far less than a buck per person per year for hundreds of millions of subsistence farmers and their households. In 2002, the US gave $3 per sub-Saharan African. Taking out the portions allocated US consultants, technical cooperation, emergency aid, administrative costs and debt relief, US aid per African was perhaps six cents.

As a signatory to global agreements like the Monterrey Consensus of 2002, the US has promised repeatedly over the decades to give a much larger proportion of its annual output, specifically up to 0.7% of GNP, to official development assistance. Its failure to follow through has no domestic political fallout, because few US citizens even know about statements like the Monterrey Consensus. But we should not underestimate the effect that failure to live up to our promises has abroad. Spin as we might about American generosity, the poor countries are fully aware of our broken promises.

The cost of action is a tiny fraction of the cost of inaction. Here are nine steps toward the goal:

COMMIT TO THE TASK: Many world leaders have embraced the goal of Making Poverty History. Now, the entire world must embrace that goal.

ADOPT A PLAN OF ACTION: The UN's Millennium Development Goals, approved by all of the world's governments, are the down payment on ending poverty. The MDGs set forth specific targets for cutting poverty, hunger, disease and environmental degradation by 2015 and thereby laid the foundation for eliminating extreme poverty by 2025. Now rich and poor countries alike must follow through.

RAISE THE VOICE OF THE POOR: Mahatma Gandhi and Martin Luther King Jr. did not wait for the rich and powerful to rescue them. They asserted their call to justice and stood steadfastly against official arrogance and neglect. It is time for democracies in the poor world to join together and issue a meaningful call to action.

REDEEM AMERICA'S ROLE IN THE WORLD: The richest, most powerful country on earth has barely participated in global efforts to end poverty, thus undermining its own security. It's time to honor our commitment to contribute 0.7% of our national income to meet this crucial goal.

RESCUE THE IMF AND WORLD BANK: They have the experience and technical sophistication to play an important role. They have the internal motivation of a highly professional staff. Yet, for many years, they have been used like debt-collection agencies for big creditor countries. It's time for them to help all 182 member countries, not just the rich ones.

STRENGTHEN THE UN: It is no use blaming the UN for missteps in the past. Why are UN agencies less operational than they should be? Not because of "UN bureaucracy," though that exists, but because powerful countries won't cede more authority. Yet UN agencies have a core role in the eradication of poverty. It is time to empower entities such as UNICEF, the World Health Organization, the Food and Agricultural Organization and many others to do their job—on the ground, country by country.

HARNESS GLOBAL SCIENCE: New technology has improved standards of living, yet science follows market forces as well as leads them. It is not surprising that the rich get richer in a continuing cycle of growth while the poorest are often left behind. Powerhouses of world science should address the unmet challenges of the poor.

PROMOTE SUSTAINABLE DEVELOPMENT: Ending extreme poverty can relieve pressure on the environment. When impoverished farmers are more productive, they stop cutting down neighboring forests. But even as extreme poverty ends, we must not fuel prosperity with industrial pollution and unchecked burning of fossil fuels.

MAKE A PERSONAL COMMITMENT: It all comes back to us. Individuals, working in unison, shape societies. Constituents do not punish politicians for helping the poor. Experience shows that the public will accept these measures, particularly if the rich bear their fair share of the burden. Great social forces are the accumulation of individual actions. Let the future say of our generation that we sent forth mighty currents of hope and worked together to heal the world.

Great social forces are the accumulation of individual actions. Let the future say of our generation that we sent forth mighty currents of hope, and that we worked together to heal the world.

IN JAKARTA, Indonesia, homeless children sleep in a train station, oblivious to the passing crowds.

A WOMAN makes her living by scavenging in a Jakarta waste dump near a new commercial development.

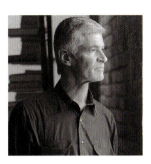

JAMES NACHTWEY

James Nachtwey (US) of *Time* magazine is the premier conflict photographer of his generation. Nachtwey has covered wars in El Salvador, Nicaragua, Israel, India, Somalia, Sudan, Rwanda, South Africa, Russia, Bosnia and Chechnya. He has received numerous honors, including six Magazine Photographer of the Year awards, five Robert Capa Gold Medals from the Overseas Press Club and two World Press Photo Awards. His searing book *Inferno* (2000) is a classic of modern photojournalism.

JEFFREY D. SACHS

Jeffrey D. Sachs (US) is the director of the Earth Institute, Quetelet Professor of Sustainable Development, and professor of health policy and management at Columbia University. He is also special advisor to UN Secretary-General Ban Ki-moon. From 2002 to 2006, he was director of the UN Millennium Project and special advisor to UN Secretary-General Kofi Annan on the Millennium Development Goals, the internationally agreed-upon goals to reduce extreme poverty, disease and hunger by the year 2015. Sachs is also president and cofounder of the Millennium Promise Alliance, a nonprofit organization aimed at ending extreme global poverty. For more than twenty years, he has been at the forefront of work on economic development, poverty alleviation, and enlightened globalization, promoting policies to help all parts of the world benefit from expanding economic opportunities and well-being. He authored *The New York Times* bestseller *The End of Poverty: Economic Possibilities for Our Time* (2005).

SHOP 'TIL WE DROP

Consumer Culture in the New Gilded Age

A YOUNG ACTRESS shops at the upscale Kirna Zabete boutique in New York.

AHH, A HOT PINK STILETTO: the perfect symbol of our culture's turn toward material excess, exclusivity and gender conformity. Sarah Jessica Parker may have incited a national obsession with Manolo Blahniks and Jimmy Choos, but many will remember Imelda Marcos and her thousand pairs long before.

How many wearers consider that a single pair costs more than the annual income of more than a billion people in the world, who live and die without access to proper food, water and shelter? This is the new gilded age, and its motto is: "If you've got it, flaunt it; if you can't afford it, borrow it; and if neither applies, you're a loser."

In the 1890s and through the Roaring Twenties—the earlier gilded age to which the current "new" refers—shoes, apparel, jewelry, automobiles, liveried servants and expensive imports were societal preoccupations. One can visit the ghostly remains at the Newport mansions or read Thorstein Veblen's biting commentary on the *riches* and *nouveau riches*. There are photos from that era as

by **JULIET B. SCHOR**

photographs by **LAUREN GREENFIELD**

well. But none are so powerful as what Lauren Greenfield has produced here. Capturing both the beauty and the horror of the conformist status symbols of our time, Greenfield's images direct our attention to four trends in consumer culture: the concentration of wealth in the hands of a small cadre of conspicuous spenders, the glorification of their lifestyle across the entire population, the incorporation of children, particularly girls, into the hyper-consumer lifestyle, and the spread of Western-style status consumption around the globe. Amid the images of ecological degradation, violence, poverty and social dysfunction that dominate this book, Greenfield's work is a mesmerizing reminder of what's behind all that pain: a system that thrives on gross inequalities and reproduces them through expensive status symbols.

The first photos in Greenfield's essay illustrate the new retailing landscape with shoes and bags. For the latter, upscale consumers now routinely pay many thousands of dollars. The bags themselves, like many other features of the lifestyle, have become supersized, by some accounts because heightened emotional insecurity has led Americans to cling ever more tightly to material objects.

The economics underlying this insecurity are grim. In the 1980s, disparities in the distributions of income and wealth began to rise dramatically. This was a reversal of a nearly fifty-year trend in which the middle class grew, poverty fell and the excesses of the first gilded age were mitigated by a progressive income tax, government social expenditures, stronger unions and more fairness in labor markets. Beginning in the late 1970s, the backlash to these policies came in the form of neoliberalism, or conservative economic policy. The most enduring impact of this shift has been a stunning rise in inequality. Over the last twenty-five years, a majority, or 60 percent, of American households have lost real income despite working longer and harder. All the gains in income went to a very small group, 5 percent of the population. And even among this rarefied segment, wealth became more concentrated. For the top 1 percent of the population, income quadrupled between 1979 and 2004. On a global scale, the richest 2 percent of adults have now amassed half the world's assets. It's a level of inequality and attendant misery unlike any the world has known.

O ver the last twenty-five years, 60 percent of American households have lost real income despite working longer and harder. All the gains in income went to the top 5 percent.

And it's what fueling the $750 stilettos, $5,000 bags, $100,000 cars and $100 million estate homes.

Why more of us haven't turned away in disgust is an interesting question. But for the most part, we haven't. The combination of celebrity culture, ubiquitous advertising, social disconnection and the cult of the new have combined to draw large segments of the population into what some contend is a pathological state of material longing. The glorification of money and its conspicuous consumption in hip-hop culture is only one example of this. Although conventional middle-class parents shake their fingers at young black stars enamored of "bling," the fact is that their own sons and daughters likely have similar tastes. Polling data shows that as a group, young people have become far more eager to be wealthy

Above:

RAPPER G-MO taping the video for his single "Ballin'." G-mo helped write the video, which is all about living large. In this scene, he counts stacks of money in his mansion in Calabasas, California.

Left:

HOLLYWOOD FILM DIRECTOR Brett Ratner (the *Rush Hour* series) and hip-hop mogul Russell Simmons weigh the relative merits of paper and plastic.

Far left:

LIL JON at his music video shoot, Los Angeles.

A TEENAGER, in her San Francisco bedroom, looks for an outfit to wear to school.

A SEVEN-YEAR-OLD BOY applies his favorite hair gel in his parents' dressing room in Malibu, California.

than ever before. In a survey I conducted some years ago of ten- to thirteen-year-olds across the socioeconomic spectrum, the statement that elicited the most enthusiastic and uniformly positive response was "I want to make a lot of money when I grow up." Little do they know that only a small percentage will achieve that goal, because wealth is a relative concept. In America in 2008, a $100,000 annual income is insufficient for many urban families to cover what are now considered "basics," a million-dollar portfolio is small potatoes, and keeping up with the Joneses has devolved into keeping up with the Gateses. By definition, the vast majority of us will be losers in this system.

Children's ambitions to be rich should come as no surprise. Greenfield's photos of young consumers reveal another trend—their participation in adultlike consumer activities almost from birth. Child-directed marketing, advertising and retailing have exploded in the last decade. In Greenfield's photos, we see girls barely beyond the toddler stage trained in expensive, sometimes painful and often time-consuming beauty rituals with which they may be saddled for the rest of their lives. By the time they reach elementary school, the most economically privileged of these girls will be adamant about their Seven jeans and Prada bags, thoroughly immersed in a media and commercial world that drives their speech patterns, values and social lives. Ten years later, according to recent accounts by psychologists who work with wealthy adolescents, they may be troubled. But for now, the five-year-old we meet at a hip upscale LA boutique in one of my favorite consumer culture images, is a discerning aesthete with a strong sense of self. I sometimes show this photo when I speak about children's commercial culture at schools. The mostly white, affluent mothers at these talks disapprove of Lily's sexually explicit clothing, but I worry that their finger-wagging is more race- and class-specific than a condemnation of the culture they inhabit.

In Greenfield's photos, gender looms large. Women have historically been the nation's consumers. They continue to do the bulk of the purchasing and are disproportionately influenced by the dictates of style and fashion. Greenfield's images are stark reminders of the normative beauty ideals that influence women of

In a survey of ten- to thirteen-year-olds across the socioeconomic spectrum, the statement that elicited the most enthusiastic and uniformly positive response was "I want to make a lot of money when I grow up."

all ages. In the first gilded age, women flocked to department stores to escape household confinement. Now, for privileged women, retail spaces may be a new prison where the consumption imperative is played out in the realm of beauty and fashion. As Betty Friedan wrote in *The Feminine Mystique*, the freedom *not* to spend is a liberation.

Aya, the sixteen-year-old whose room is strewn with clothing, represents the other side of the consumer equation. While the rich busy themselves acquiring items whose prices are so stratospheric they're the stuff of science fiction, the average American has participated in the consumer boom through the proliferation of cheap stuff. Apparel is the canonical case. From the early 1990s until now, average apparel prices have declined precipitously, courtesy (mostly) of women in Asian sweatshops. Outlets such as Old Navy and H&M now offer trendy styles at "you can afford to wear it once" prices. Thanks to new information technology, the chains can replicate styles from the New York and Paris runways and put these garments in stores in a matter of weeks. And that's about as long as they stay on the racks (in contrast to an earlier world of climatically driven apparel seasons). By 2005, the average US consumer was buying more than one new item of apparel every week, an increase of more than 80 percent in fifteen years.

Similar trends characterize other consumer categories. Exploitive labor conditions and failure to pass the environmental costs of production and transport on to the consumer have resulted in unrealistically cheap imported goods and a sharp rise in the quantities purchased by US consumers. This pattern holds true for consumer electronics, household items such as dishes and glasses, furniture, jewelry, sporting goods, rugs, small appliances and a wide range of other miscellaneous products. The one major exception is footwear, most likely because Nike, with its prodigious brand appeal, has been able to stave off H&M-style competitors and keep the ratio of sales price to manufacturing cost sky-high.

The final stage of this "fashion cycle" is discard. Even the dramatic expansion in upper- and upper-middle-class home size, along with the proliferation of walk-in closets, extra garages and rental storage facilities, hasn't kept up with the mountains of con-

Following pages, clockwise from top left:
A TWO-YEAR-OLD gets a pedicure from an "aesthetician," while her mom, Beverly, looks on at the Spahhht Youth Spa at the Hyatt Regency Hill Country Resort & Spa in San Antonio, Texas.

SHOPPING at Rachel London's Garden in Los Angeles, where pop singer Britney Spears has some of her clothes designed.

A THREE-YEAR-OLD at the VIP opening of Barneys department store in Beverly Hills.

PRIVILEGED youth in Milan, Italy, hold piles of clothes and shoes while shopping in the swank Corso Vittorio Emanuele district.

WINDOW-SHOPPING on Rodeo Drive.

sumer goods accumulating in American homes. There's no room for all this stuff, so we're discarding it—to charities, curbside collection or the dump. There is now a vigorous international trade in used American garments. Gap T-shirts and last year's jeans return to the poor countries where they were made, to be worn by those whose wages are too low to afford indigenously produced apparel. It's another dysfunctional circuit of the global capitalist economy.

The continuation of this mad economic model is now in doubt, as the falling dollar and rising oil prices have undermined its fundamentals. And even if the model were still economically sustainable, the ecological havoc it has wreaked on the climate and the world's ecosystems is not. We can see these environmental effects in other chapters of this book—the devastation of China's natural

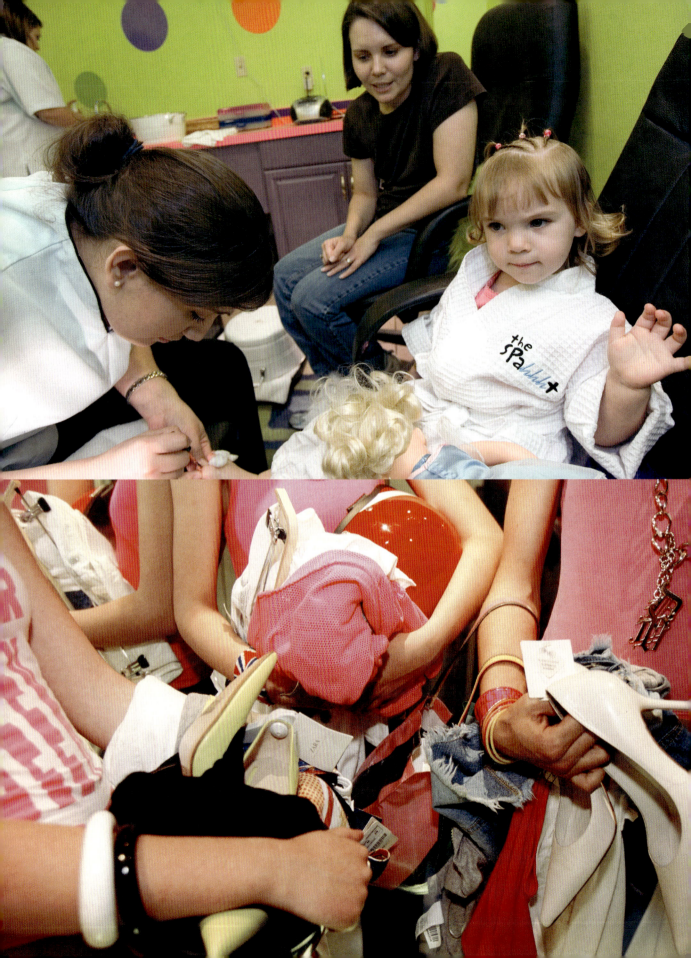

YVONNE XUE, 44, board chairman and general manager of Shanghai Si Tong Cable Industry and vice board chairman of Shanghai Huiyang Industry Company, in her Versace-designed bedroom in Shanghai.

ZHANG YU CHEN, owner and developer of the Beijing Laffitte Chateau, in one of the hotel's many private dining rooms.

systems, global warming created by overconsumption, and the degradation of the oil and extractive economies.

The photos in this chapter end with wealth and status displays in East Asia—in both their historic form, in which elites consume ostentatiously, and a contemporary version, in which a growing upper middle class replicates the lifestyle of their Western counterparts: designer furniture, BMWs and golf attire. The spread of consumerism is a global story, but Asia is quickly becoming the epicenter, a development brilliantly illustrated by Greenfield's photo of a female executive in Shanghai. While her lavish bedroom suggests the allure of the global luxury market, her vigor symbolizes the rise of the Asian economies. By contrast, the relaxed decadence of the photos shot in America suggest an empire in decline. Perhaps there's a moral here after all.

CHU XIANG YU and her husband, Cai Min, live in the Long Island Villas, a subdivision outside of Shanghai.

Previous pages:
SENIORS from Newport High School in Orange County, California, socialize on the party bus taking them to their senior prom.

S. W. LAM, owner of 3-D Gold, sitting on his company's solid gold toilet.

LAUREN GREENFIELD

Author of the critically acclaimed books *Fast Forward*, *Girl Culture* and *Thin*, Lauren Greenfield (US) was named by *American Photo* as one of the twenty-five most influential photographers working today. She is a member of the VII Photo Agency, and her work appears regularly in *The New York Times Magazine*, *Time* and *Elle*. It is also in many public and private collections, including those of the San Francisco Museum of Modern Art and the Art Institute of Chicago. Greenfield's honors include the ICP Infinity Award and a Hasselblad Foundation grant. Her first documentary, *Thin*, broadcast on HBO, earned her an Emmy nomination for Best Direction. *Thin* premiered at the Sundance Film Festival in 2006 and won the Grand Jury Prize at the London Film Festival. Her latest film, *kids + money*, was selected for the 2008 Sundance Film Festival, won the Audience Award at the AFI Film Festival and will also be broadcast on HBO.

JULIET B. SCHOR

Juliet B. Schor (US) is a professor of sociology at Boston College and author of the forthcoming *Consumerism and Its Discontents* as well as *Born to Buy: The Commercialized Child and the New Consumer Culture*. She also wrote *The New York Times* bestseller *The Overworked American: The Unexpected Decline of Leisure* and *The Overspent American*. A former Guggenheim Fellow, Schor received the Leontief Prize in 2006 for "advancing the frontiers of economic knowledge." She is a cofounder and currently cochair of the board of directors of the Center for a New American Dream. She appears frequently on television and radio, and has been profiled by *The New York Times, The Wall Street Journal, Newsweek* and *People*, among other publications. Prior to joining Boston College, she spent seventeen years on the faculty at Harvard University.

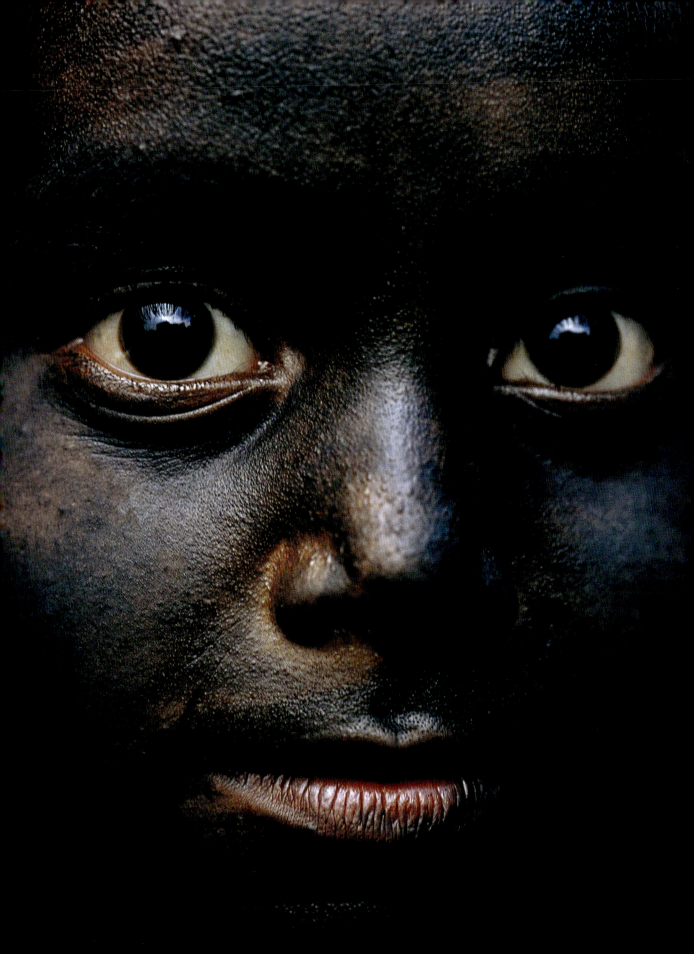

CHILDREN OF THE BLACK DUST
Child Labor in Bangladesh

SATHI'S FACE is covered with carbon dust from recycled batteries. She is eight years old and works in a battery recycling factory in Korar Ghat, on the outskirts of Dhaka, Bangladesh.

AS SHE CLEANS THE CARBON RODS from exhausted D-cell batteries, Marjina holds her young child on her lap and gently lulls her to sleep. Marjina migrated from the countryside to Dhaka, the capital of Bangladesh, with her son and four daughters after her husband died. Now she toils every day in a workshop by the Buriganga River that recycles used batteries. Wiping tears from her eyes, Marjina tells me, "Regardless of how hard my children and I work, we accumulate more and more debt every month. I don't know what to do. I have nothing that I can sell to pay off my debts."

In my country, Bangladesh, labor comes cheap. On the outskirts of Dhaka, in village-like slums, dozens of workshops recycle the cast-off materials scavenged from garbage dumps. One of these unnamed workshops recycles dry-cell batteries. Day in and day out, women and children as young as three or four break open discarded batteries with hammers in order to remove the recyclable

photographs and text by **SHEHZAD NOORANI**

carbon rods and tiny pieces of reusable metal. Depending upon the speed of their work, they earn between 30 and 50 taka (40 to 70 US cents) per day. For a young child, it often takes more than a week to earn the equivalent of one US dollar.

Like Marjina, many women bring their children to work because there is simply no other place for them to stay. The environment in and around the workshops is loaded with carbon dust and other toxic material. Young children play in these polluted areas until they are tired and fall asleep, and most suffer from chest and eye infections.

Working conditions in these workshops are dismal and depressing. The makeshift cabins are often lit by one sixty-watt bulb or a single small window. The hours are long, the work tedious, and everything—walls, ceilings and even the children's faces—is covered with black carbon dust. Often only the whites of their eyes and red shiny lips are visible. The children constantly lick their lips to keep them wet, literally eating the dust particles. The particles they inhale can lead to black lung disease.

It is easy to dramatize the plight of these young workers in order to create a sensational report. As you can see from my photographs on these pages, the visuals are horrific. But I always try to be careful, because as hard as it is to imagine, I know that sensational reports in the media can actually create even worse situations for these children.

Child labor, as UNICEF's annual *State of the World's Children* report explains, is a complex and often misunderstood problem, but here are some of the basic facts: An estimated 250 million children are employed around the world. Of these, nearly three-quarters, or 170 million, work under hazardous conditions—in mines, with chemicals and pesticides, or operating dangerous machinery. Although child laborers are ubiquitous, they are often virtually invisible, toiling as domestic servants in homes, hidden from view on plantations or, in the case of Marjina's children, covered in black carbon dust behind the walls of an anonymous workshop.

While not unique among South Asian countries, Bangladesh may present the world's most gruesome picture of the rich openly and grossly exploiting the poor. While economic inequities exist

A young child often takes more than a week to earn the equivalent of one US dollar.

BATTERY RECYCLERS
in Dhaka.

to a greater or lesser degree in every nation, in Bangladesh the inequality between haves and have-nots is startling and unabashed. It strikes me whenever I see drivers in BMWs, Mercedes and Hummers on the streets of Dhaka, raving and honking behind man-powered cycle rickshaws pulling heavy loads. And as in the rest of South Asia, you can't help but notice the hideous slums that butt up against fancy upper-middle-class apartment blocks. There is no serviceable separation of the classes here.

Open space is almost nonexistent in Dhaka. Regularly battered by natural disasters such as floods, cyclones and resultant soil erosion—worsening now in the age of global warming—desperate

USING WATER pumped from the Buriganga River, a young girl washes carbon rods from used batteries at a battery recycling workshop in Ayena Ghat, Bangladesh.

rural families are migrating to urban areas at an astonishing rate, overwhelming city services. In the last decade, Dhaka has become one of the most densely populated cities in the world. Many rural families move to the cities out of desperation, hoping for better employment opportunities, only to find themselves spiraling deeper into debt with nowhere to turn.

In addition to natural calamities, one of the major causes of Bangladesh's mounting poverty is a lack of government investment in the social sector. This is largely due to the unnatural calamity of corruption that reaches into every imaginable government office. In 2005, for the fifth year in a row, Bangladesh was at the very bottom of Transparency International's Corruption Perception Index. In 2006, it was third from the bottom.

"Corruption is a major cause of poverty as well as a barrier to overcoming it," explains Transparency International chairman Peter Eigen. "The two scourges feed off each other, locking their populations in a cycle of misery."

Government corruption and the resultant cycle of poverty have a direct and calamitous impact on the welfare of Bangladeshi children. More than seven million children work in Bangladesh—many from 6 a.m. until 7 p.m.—scavenging heaps of garbage, hammering and breaking bricks under the burning heat, melting and molding metal in workshops. They work thirteen hours just so they can have one decent meal at the end of the day. Their wages are paltry, practically nonexistent. They are exposed to hazards that are inconceivable to most of us.

The sad fact is that these children have to work to stay alive; if they don't work, they don't eat. But, that does not mean that they have to be exploited. In Bangladesh, with one of the largest collections of nongovernmental organizations and international agencies in the world, it is shameful that millions of my countrymen live on the edge of extinction.

But the world being the way it is, and Bangladesh being Bangladesh, I am convinced that no agency or government will be able to fix this situation until there is an economic solution that benefits businesses as well as children. For example, the major export-based industry of Bangladesh, the garment industry, once employed thousands of children. Generally, they were given low-skill tasks such as cutting and trimming loose threads from completed garments. They helped the sewing machine operators and the finishers who packed the products. The garment industry benefited from cheap child labor, and there was a visible positive effect on the entire society.

But all of this came to an abrupt halt in 1992 when Democratic senator Tom Harkin of Iowa introduced the well-meaning Child Labor Deterrence Act. Also known as the Harkin Bill, it threatened to ban importation of garments from developing countries that employ child labor. Fearing loss of substantial business from US buyers, frightened garment companies in Bangladesh quickly fired more than 50,000 child workers. A UNICEF study later concluded that these unemployed children were, for the most part, forced into other work that was often far more dangerous and less lucrative—breaking rocks, rolling cigarettes, working construction and engaging in prostitution.

This is what concerns me about publishing photographs such as the ones you see here. Seeing images of children working in dangerous conditions for little or no pay, making goods for Western consumers, leaves those consumers with a sense of guilt and powerlessness. The resulting boycotts ease the conscience of the consumers but actually harm the children they seek to protect. While children can be exploited and abused in all forms of employment, it is the larger establishments, such as the Bangladeshi garment factories, that allow monitoring and control blatant abuse. In relatively decent settings like garment factories, systems can be put in place that ensure some form of education, life-skill training and decent pay. Once the children are thrown out of the garment factories, all that is thrown out with them.

As Shahidul Alam, a photojournalist and a social activist in Dhaka, explains, "The notion that a garment employer might be helping children by allowing them to work may seem very strange to people in the West. But in a country where the majority of people live in villages, where children work in the home and the fields as part of growing up, there are no romantic notions of childhood as an age of innocence."

These children have to work to stay alive; if they don't work, they don't eat.

Not all child work is harmful. Some children actually choose to work, to develop new skills and move toward adulthood. Millions of children work part-time, combining work with school. Often children's wages make the difference between destitution and survival for their families. Take away their jobs and children go hungry, become homeless or are driven to more poorly paid, more dangerous jobs.

Harunur Rashid, a battery recycling plant owner, replied, "When the government forbids employment of children, what happens to the families going hungry? The law itself is good, but you have to be practical."

As horrible as all this may sound, it is important to understand that, for many children, earning a living or supplementing their family's income is a matter of survival. Slogans like "Stop Child Labor" embody romantic and ultimately impractical notions when it comes to places like Bangladesh. Instead of trying to abolish child labor by boycotting goods made by children, governments and civil societies should help create safer working environments for children, ensure that systems are in place to monitor abuse, and provide education and a living wage.

The Amsterdam Conference on Child Labour in 1997, which included young delegates—working children from Central and South America, West Africa and Asia—concluded, "Action should be taken to eradicate the most pernicious forms of child labor. But, in the absence of a real assault on the root causes of poverty, children should have the right to work. It is not work but exploitation in the workplace that should be targeted." Until that happens, children will be living and dying in the conditions you see here.

Slogans like "Stop Child Labor" embody romantic and ultimately impractical notions when it comes to places like Bangladesh.

RENA AYNOL, 19, recycles AA batteries. She has been working in the recycling shop since she was eleven.

A WOMAN HOLDS HER CHILD, who is blackened by carbon dust. His nose bleeds from infections caused by exposure to carbon dust and other pollutants.

PERVAIZ, 11, works in a blacksmith workshop making brass bells that classical Indian dancers wear on their feet while performing.

A THREE-YEAR-OLD girl sits on the window ledge of the battery recycling workshop where she works.

SHEHZAD NOORANI

Shehzad Noorani (Bangladesh) has worked as a freelance documentary photographer since 1987. His special focus is people who live on the lowest rung of the socioeconomic ladder. He has covered major crises resulting from wars and natural calamities in Afghanistan, Iraq, Sudan, Uganda, Sri Lanka, Iran and Bangladesh. Other assignments for agencies such as UNICEF have taken him to more than thirty countries. Noorani has also edited photographs for numerous publications. His work has appeared in *Geo*, *Newsweek*, *The New York Times*, *Le Monde*, *The Guardian* and *The British Journal of Photography* and has been exhibited widely around the world. For *Daughters of Darkness*, his project on the lives of commercial sex workers, he received the Mother Jones International Fund for Documentary Photography Award in 2000.

AN INFANT SLEEPS on a jute bag. His mother works in the battery recycling factory and brings him along so she can look after him while she works.

LOST GIRLS
The Child Brides of Afghanistan, Nepal & Ethiopia

A "LOST TRIBE" often describes an ethnic group dispersed in time or the lost portion of a grand heritage or religion. But there are other ways to get lost. Many girls in the poorest communities of the poorest countries of the developing world are lost as children to a state sanctified and validated as "marriage."

In the next ten years, if present patterns continue, more than 100 million girls will be married as children. Child brides can be found all over the world, from Nepal, India, Afghanistan and Bangladesh to Mozambique and West Africa—which has the highest rates of child marriage in the world—to the marginalized indigenous populations of Latin America, such as the Mayan Highlands and the rural areas of the Dominican Republic. In some Ethiopian districts, nearly half of the girls are married off by age fifteen. One hundred million is a difficult number to comprehend, and it makes it difficult to think of all these girls as individual humans with hopes, dreams and aspirations, but if you look at Stephanie Sinclair's moving photographs of child brides on these pages, you get a better idea of the problem.

by **JUDITH BRUCE**
photographs by **STEPHANIE SINCLAIR**

SOON-TO-BE-WED Faiz Mohammed, 40, and Ghulam Haider, 11, at Ghulam's home in the rural village of Damarda in Ghowr Province, Afghanistan.

Child marriage is probably the most common regularly occurring, socially approved human rights abuse in the world today.

Child marriage fits most of the criteria for enslavement established by Anti-Slavery International: child brides are forced to work and serve others under the threat of mental or physical punishment; they are dehumanized; they are treated as property; their movements are severely restricted; and, most crushingly, their futures are obliterated.

Child marriage has traditionally been an invisible issue in the international policy arena. Trend data homogenizes experience, and we're told that across the world "the age at marriage is increasing." National-level information also shows an upward trend in the marriage age, but both these figures hide vast internal differentials. The belief persists among urban elites—based on their own experience—that child marriage is rare, and that to the extent that it persists, it is residual and confined to small populations. The continuation of this custom is often viewed as a negligible human rights abuse. But, in fact, child marriage is probably the most common regularly occurring, socially approved human rights abuse in the world today—an abuse that directly causes higher than necessary maternal mortality, infant mortality, intergenerational poverty and, increasingly, the spread of HIV.

These girls are lost not only to themselves but to their communities and their nations. Their loss is typically abrupt and comprehensive. They often learn of their marriage on the day itself. In

MEENA ACHARYA, 15, cries as she recounts her experience as a child bride at the Child Workers in Nepal Concerned Centre (CWIN), which helped her since she ran away from her husband a year earlier.

short order, their bodies are appropriated by others—for uncompensated labor, for unprotected and coercive sexual pleasure and for the production of children, which is the price of a secure marriage. Girls married as children, like girls trafficked into social slavery or those inducted into domestic service, experience the sudden and definitive end of childhood.

On the heels of child marriage comes child motherhood, usually the result of a physically or socially forced sexual relationship. The girl has nine months to anxiously anticipate a birth that will likely take place without benefit of appropriate medical support and which is sometimes completely unattended. Maternal mortality and physical damage such as obstetrical fistula, which is related to a long, unproductive labor in a small, underdeveloped pelvis, is increasingly concentrated among the youngest first-time mothers.

Child marriage is also increasingly associated with HIV. The child bride in the context of an HIV epidemic encounters a perfect storm of risk. Usually, the younger the bride, the larger the age differential with her spouse, and this age gap matters. The older the man, the more likely he is to have had previous sexual relations, increasing the probability that he has acquired HIV.

The greatest loss, however, may be not physical but social. A child bride is typically not in school. Marriage occasionally necessitates leaving school, but usually families don't invest in these girls,

TSEGAYA MEKONEN, 13, prepares to meet her groom, Talema Meseret, 23, on their wedding day in Ethiopia. The practice of early marriage remains widespread in Ethiopia, especially in the northern Amhara and Tigray regions, where parents consent to consummated marriages when their daughters are as young as ten.

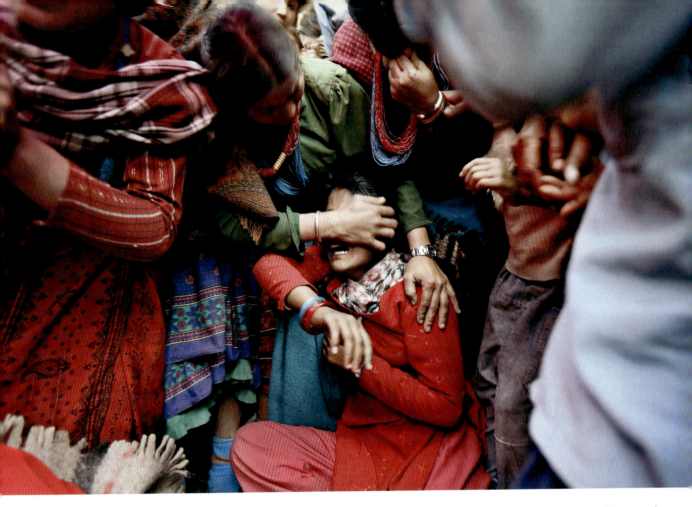

IN NEPAL, Saraswati Shreshta Balami, 14, cries as the groom's family takes her sister, Sumeena Shreshta Balami, 15, away.

so they have little or no schooling. Her marriage usually entails moving to a new household and often an entirely new community. There, she has very few friends because she lacks the social power to meet them. She has no place outside the home where she can have privacy or fun. (Remember, she is still a child.) Even though she is probably the most vulnerable potential mother in the world, she usually has no access to media, social messaging or modern health care.

The lost girl reemerges as a visible social entity, if at all, only when she has given birth to several surviving children, including, ideally, some boys. Only these children provide her with some standing in the community and elevated negotiating power over resources and sexual relations with her husband. And, critically, her children give her some company. The great value that a child bride places on her children is no surprise; they are her closest allies in life.

We must eliminate child marriage, in all of its forms, in all parts of the world, wherever it takes place, and we must do it now.

Fortunately, there is hope. Most countries have a favorable framework of laws defining the age of consent as either sixteen or eighteen. Most are signatories to the Convention on the Rights of the Child (CRC) or the Convention on the Elimination of All Forms of Discrimination Against Women (CEDAW), both of which define eighteen as the legal age of consent and marriage. In many poor communities there is a new and growing understanding that keeping girls out of school and compelling them into early marriage and childbearing reduces economic and social benefits for everyone. But religious, civil and governmental leaders need to enact explicit programs and incentives. The girls need health and birth certificates that establish their age and protect against child marriage. They need economic skills, viable opportunities, knowledge of their rights and the power to claim them. They need to stay in school through adolescence. Crucially, they need safe places to meet and identify with other girls, the support of friends and mentors, and a proud female identity bonded to other females.

PURNIMA SHRESHTA BALAMI, 15, is prepared for her wedding, though she does not yet know that. Purnima was told she would marry the sun god, a Newari cultural tradition. When she eventually met her young groom at the wedding ceremony, she refused to marry him and ran away.

Investment in these girls and young women has huge and unexpected returns.

Top:

A NEWLY MARRIED couple in their home in Nepal's Terai region, where girls are often married to their groom as small children, then later have a second celebration called *a gonar*, after which the girl moves into the husband's home and assumes her marital duties.

Bottom:

SURITA SHRESHTA BALAMI, 16, at her new home in Nepal after her marriage.

In those areas where change will take more time, there are still things that can be done. Programs on the ground can encourage later marriage by explicitly informing these girls' parents about safe, legal marriage and that an older husband is not always a good choice. These programs can help parents understand the links between maternal and infant health and disabuse them of the notion that they are doing anything to "protect" their daughters by marrying them off—a particular paradox in the age of HIV.

There are also more than 50 million girls and young women, aged eighteen to twenty-four, who were married as children and who can be retrieved. They also need a social identity, personal documentation, friendships and a place to meet their friends. They too can become literate, learn basic financial management, develop livelihood skills, have personal savings under their own control, and develop the knowledge to protect their health and that of their children. They too can be safe and valued by their communities.

Investment in these girls and young women has huge and unexpected returns. Many years ago, I interviewed the founding head of the Nepal Women's Organization, Mrs. Kamal Dhunhana. Kamal was taken from her parents to the distant home of her husband and married at age eleven. During an interview at the first Women's Conference in Mexico City in 1975, she told me, eyes glistening, that she loved her parents deeply and had been terrified to leave. Her father was the poet laureate of Nepal, yet she was illiterate. In her new home, she saw her husband reading and desperately begged him to teach her.

When she learned to read it was a revolution, but not only for her. She said, "I knew if I could learn to read, I could learn to do anything." She went on to establish the Nepali Women's Organization—11,000 strong—which advocates for girls' education and women's rights, including the right to choose the number and timing of their own children and a role for women in village councils and even the Nepali parliament.

All that came from teaching one child bride to read. We can only imagine what might be accomplished by the 100 million girls who will be lost to child marriage in the next ten years if we don't act now.

IN ETHIOPIA, Tsegaya Mekonen, 13, and Talema Meseret, 23, sit together as husband and wife for the first time.

MOHAMMED FAZAL, 45, with his two wives, Majabin, 13, and Zalayha, 29, in a village on the outskirts of Mazar-e-Sharif, Afghanistan. Majabin's father offered her up as settlement when he could not pay his gambling debt after a night of cards.

A YOUNG PROSTITUTE
stunned after being beaten
by a customer. Many of the
girls who run away from
child marriages in Ethiopia
end up in brothels, where
they are physically abused.

SAID MOHAMMED, 55,
and Roshan Kasem, 8, on
the day of their engagement
in the village of Chavosh in
Ghowr Province, Afghanistan.
The father of the bride,
Abdul Kasem, 60, says he
does not want to give his
daughter away at such a
young age, but he cannot
afford to keep her.

STEPHANIE SINCLAIR

Stephanie Sinclair (US), based in Beirut, Lebanon, is known for her work on gender issues and human rights. Her clients include *The New York Times Magazine*, *German Geo*, *Stern*, *Time*, *Newsweek* and *Marie Claire*. In 2007, Sinclair was named UNICEF Photographer of the Year for her work on child marriage. Her work has also been recognized by The Visa Pour L'Image festival in France, the World Press Photo Foundation and FiftyCrows International Fund for Documentary Photography. While on the staff of the *Chicago Tribune*, Sinclair was awarded a Chicago Bar Association award for work on the Illinois death penalty that resulted in a state moratorium on capital punishment. She was also part of the *Tribune* team that won the 2000 Pulitzer Prize for documenting problems in the airline industry.

FEMALE FAMILY MEMBERS in Afghanistan mourn Shakila Ramani, who died after self-immolating and burning 95 percent of her body during a fight with her husband and in-laws. She left behind two young children.

JUDITH BRUCE

Judith Bruce (US) is a senior associate and policy analyst in the Population Council's Poverty, Gender, and Youth program. Since joining the council in 1977, she has coordinated policy-oriented research on issues related to women's and adolescent girls' social and economic development. A longtime member of the Council on Foreign Relations, Bruce received the Association for Women in Development's biannual award for outstanding contributions to the field. A Harvard graduate, she has written and lectured extensively on population policy, reproductive health services and adolescent girls in the developing world. She called early attention to child marriage and the situation of married adolescent girls with articles and publications including "The Unchartered Passage: Girls' Adolescence in the Developing World," "Married Adolescent Girls: Human Rights, Health, and Developmental Needs of a Neglected Majority" and "Protecting Young Women from HIV/AIDS: The Case Against Child and Adolescent Marriage."

THE PRICE OF OUR OIL ADDICTION

Scenes from the Niger River Delta

WORKERS PUSH gasoline barrels from the water-front onto the main market road of Yenagoa, Nigeria.

ADDICTION EXPOSES THE DEEPEST FORMS OF PHYSICAL AND PSYCHOLOGICAL DEPENDENCY. It is typically considered a personal affliction or an individual failing. But the deadly solicitations of any addictive substance—cocaine, alcohol, nicotine—rely upon a social, economic, and political infrastructure. The great behavioral scientist Gregory Bateson, who studied addiction at the Langley Porter Institute in San Francisco during the 1950s, drew an analogy between the addict and a runaway car precisely to highlight the "system of addiction." He wrote:

"The panic of the alcoholic who has hit bottom is the panic of the man who thought he had control over a vehicle but suddenly finds that the vehicle can run away with him. Suddenly, pressure on what he knows is the brake seems to make the vehicle go faster. It is the panic of discovering that *it* (the system, self *plus* vehicle) is bigger than he is. . . . He has bankrupted the epistemology of 'self-control.'"

by **MICHAEL WATTS**
photographs by **ED KASHI**

The irrefutable reality is that more growth—the primary objective of capitalism—means burning more fossil fuel.

The crack addict needs the dealer; the trafficker needs the producer; and each is embedded in an immense empire of shady government officials, mules, cartel acolytes and peasant growers, as well as a vast shadow world of drug barons, security forces and corrupt governments. There are those—social psychologist Stanton Peele is one—who believe that addiction has become an epidemic of modern society. Addiction, says Peele, "is not . . . an aberration from our way of life. . . . [It] is our way of life." Addiction industries enable and pathologize all manner of behaviors—from shopping to gambling to drinking to the Internet. Addiction, in other words, is a peculiarly modern condition, the loss of both personal *and* social control. Some addictions are deep, structural and radically destructive; they expose the morbidities of modern life and of modern capitalism.

There is no better place to read about the pathologies of contemporary addiction than William Burroughs' *Naked Lunch*. For Burroughs, a longtime opiate addict, drug addiction is part of a "junk economy" in which the "junk virus" is a parasitic organism that invades and controls increasingly compliant subjects. In Burroughs' world, drugs produce a "grotesque consumer" reduced to one "overpowering bodily need." Life, he says, telescopes down to one fix. Drugs are the "ideal merchandise": no sales talk necessary. The pusher does not sell drugs to the consumer; the consumer sells himself to the product. The addict knows no limit, no control; he is the capitalist consumer par excellence. He would, says Burroughs, "lie, cheat, inform on friends, steal, do anything to satisfy total need." In Burroughs' universe, the junk economy is ingrained in a wider economy of control in which the human body is subject to all manner of parasites that multiply in large bureaucracies, complex technologies and multifarious social organizations. The individual human body, under siege from a "vast hungry host of parasites," is reduced to what Burroughs calls "a soft machine."

Burroughs depicts a terminal capitalist world: the deadly deceits of the market, big business, state control and technological terror, and the mass production of mindless subjects. It is a dark, dystopian vision, but one that speaks directly to the realities that surround us: chronic dependency, demand without limits, violent

acquisition and addictive control. One of these realities is the energy system—hydrocarbons in general, and oil and gas in particular—that undergirds our modern way of life.

I want to pose the following question: Is our dependence on oil a sort of addiction? What is the symptomology of petro-addiction, and what are its social costs? Is oil, to return to Burroughs, *the* ideal commodity for neoliberal free-market capitalism? Have vehicularized and, increasingly, sport-utilitized American consumers become Burroughs' archetypical soft machines, beset and enslaved by hydrocarbon capitalism?

We could begin with President George W. Bush's 2006 State of the Union address. America, he said, is "addicted to oil, which is often imported from unstable parts of the world." As a former oilman and a former alcoholic, he should know oil addiction when he sees it. Five years earlier, Vice President Dick Cheney's National Energy Policy report deployed another word from the lexicon of addiction: Americans' oil fix could be obtained only through "a *dependency* on foreign powers that do not have America's interests at heart" (my emphasis). What neither man admitted was that America's oil addiction rested upon a post–World War II "global oil acquisition

IN RIVERS STATE, a Chinese contractor from ZPED works with Nigerians and the French oil company Total to drill for natural gas. Total has operated in the Niger Delta since 1968. This is its 125th well.

Left and right:
WORKERS HIRED
by Shell Petroleum
Development Company
clean up an oil spill
from an abandoned well
in Oloibiri.

strategy"—the language is from Michael Klare's book *Blood and Oil*—that now lay in ruins. America's oil strategy, a central tenet of US foreign policy since President Roosevelt met King Saud aboard the USS *Quincy* in 1945 and cobbled together their "special relationship," succeeded in fueling the low-cost, motorized American way of life. But the true costs of cheap oil—a vast military presence in the Middle East; environmental damage, including global climate change; the need to support corrupt "oilygarchs"—have never been paid by consumers at the fuel pump. And a half century of "special relationships"—or, more precisely, addictive codependencies—have only produced Venezuela's Hugo Chavez, Libya's Muammar al-Gaddafi, Iran's Mahmoud Ahmadinejad and, in the end, September 11, Osama bin Laden's murderous response to the permanent deployment of American troops in the oil-rich Saudi holy land.

OPEC's surplus capacity is currently at an all-time low; there is a deep suspicion that so-called booked reserves—estimates of recoverable oil—may be inflated fictions. Newly motorized economies in India and China need a growing portion of world oil production. Speculation runs rampant in commodity exchanges, stoked by political turmoil and conflict in many oil-producing states and by "resource nationalism" emboldened by the high

prices. The price of oil rises on fear and conflict, so petro-states can raise the cost virtually at will by provoking crises and conflicts—usually with the United States.

As a result, international oil companies, national oil companies, and oil-producing states are awash in money. Their profits are unprecedented. ExxonMobil, the largest of the international oil companies, has a market valuation of nearly $450 billion, or slightly more than the entire GDP of sub-Saharan Africa. In 2007, it booked a net profit of more than $40 billion, which translates to a stack of dollar bills more than 10,000 miles high. The national oil companies—the so-called New Titans that account for 90 percent of global oil reserves and more than one-third of output—are equally flush. But to all intents and purposes, they are black boxes—massively corrupt, completely unaccountable and poorly managed. One commentator described the Venezuelan national oil company (PDVSA) as "a party with the lights out and the music on full blast." In 2007, the OPEC states alone raked in a staggering $688 billion. The Gulf countries each bank roughly $5 billion a week. Hey, addiction pays.

We are now in the midst of the third great oil boom (the first two being 1973–74 and 1979–80). Like previous booms, the current one has transferred unimaginable wealth from oil-importing to oil-producing countries, and from consumers to oil companies. But the current oil crisis, set against the Global War on Terror, has two novel characteristics. One is the vast wealth of oil-producing states in a global industry where the best and largest assets are not in the hands of what the *Economist* calls "the most efficient and best capitalized firms," namely the major oil companies. The other is the rank complicity of the American empire, militarism and corporate power. Not only did a former oilman (surrounded by a posse of other former oilmen) stalk the halls of the White House for eight years, but as Kevin Phillips writes in *American Theocracy*, oil now stands at the summit of American politics and "an oil, automobile, and national-security coalition has taken the driver's seat."

Contemporary talk of the end of cheap and easy oil—and the surge of oil prices to more than $100 per barrel—reminds us of the 1973 OPEC oil embargo and President Nixon's "Project Independence," designed to achieve US self-sufficiency by 1980. For the record, US dependency on imported oil in the late 1960s was 20 percent; it is expected to be about 66 percent by 2025. Nixon's policy failed miserably, and he resorted to enhancing domestic supply at a terrifying environmental cost and by turning to reliable low-cost foreign suppliers.

"Oil security"—through unconventional oil sources, enhanced oil-recovery and "green fields" (i.e., previously untapped oil fields; nothing "green" about them)—were also talking points thirty years later in the Cheney report. Alternative energy sources and energy conservation (both of which would "compromise the American way of life," as George Bush père put it at the Rio conference on the environment in 1992) barely warranted a mention. Cheney's motto was always "go where the oil is." In 2005, that meant drilling in the pristine Arctic National Wildlife Refuge, Wyoming, and Azerbaijan, and raping the vast tar-sands of northern Alberta.

But nowhere has America pursued its search for new oil with more ferocity and dedication than the west coast of Africa, particularly the Gulf of Guinea. African oil production along the Atlantic littoral has attracted huge exploration investment, and the region will contribute more than 30 percent of the world's increase in liquid hydrocarbon production by 2010. During the last five years, when undiscovered oil fields have become a scarce commodity, Africa has contributed one in every four barrels of new petroleum discovered outside North America. Africa is Big Oil's new battleground. Former oilman Jeremy Leggett writes in his book *The Empty Tank* that energy security has three legs: "The Empire of Oil," "The Culture of Suppression," and "The Great Addiction." Ed Kashi's photographs of the Niger Delta—one of Africa's frontier oil regions—capture, more powerfully than words, the ugly, violent on-the-ground realities of Leggett's Holy Trinity at work.

What is the true nature of oil dependency? More than 150 million years ago, massive blooms of microscopic marine plants created a huge blanket of organic material on the sea floor. In some locations, sedimentation created sufficient pressure to convert—to cook—the unoxidized carbon in the organic material into oil, some of which was trapped in reservoirs. A second phase of oil formation occurred 90 million years ago. Most oil stayed put until its discovery in 1859. With the invention of the gas-fueled automobile in 1901, black gold became the drug of choice, and its ascent marked the coming of Big Oil. By the time Sinclair Lewis wrote his novel *Oil!* in 1927, the corruption, violence, corporate power and pure ambition that became the oil industry's hallmarks were already in place in California. Eighty years later, 90 percent of our transportation is fueled by oil; 90 percent of all goods involve oil in some way; and 95 percent of our food products require oil. (To raise one cow and deliver it to market requires more than 250 gallons of oil.) Globally, the world consumes more than 80 million barrels every day; the United States alone accounts for one-quarter of that. According to most industry expectations, by 2025 global oil consumption will increase by more than 50 percent. Exactly where this oil will come from is unclear. The irrefutable reality is that more growth—the primary objective of capitalism—means burning more fossil fuel.

Petro-addiction is in large measure an obsession with the automobile and mobility. The vast corporate nexus of the oil, automobile, and petrochemical industries—enabled by the military and political power of the American imperial state—constitutes the system of addiction. In 1900, 57 percent of all US-refined

Nowhere has America pursued its search for new oil with more ferocity and dedication than the west coast of Africa, particularly the Gulf of Guinea.

DAILY LIFE in Finima,
a community of displaced
people set in the shadow
of the ExxonMobil gas plant
on Bonny Island.

A WOMAN carrying a Shell
Oil umbrella traverses the
Nigerian National Petroleum
pipeline in the Okrika
district near Port Harcourt.

America's initial response to September 11 was slapping flag stickers on SUVs and buying Hummers.

petroleum was used in kerosene lamps. By 1930, nearly half was consumed by cars. In the same year, there were 143,000 gasoline stations, 219 vehicles for every 1,000 Americans, and an auto industry capable of absorbing 80 percent of all rubber, 75 percent of all glass, and a quarter of all steel.

Private automobiles now account for more than half of all US oil consumption, and the transportation sector as a whole uses almost three-quarters. Two-thirds of this oil is imported. There are now more than 250 million registered vehicles in the United States, one for every 1.2 Americans; and more than 17 million new vehicles are sold annually. The growth sector for the last quarter century has been light trucks, a category in which fuel efficiency has deteriorated over time. The number of gas-guzzling SUVs has grown steadily, from 2 percent of the market in 1975 to more than 25 percent in 2003. America's immediate response to September 11 was slapping flag stickers on SUVs and buying Hummers. Oil profligacy is the end result of a century-long addiction to motorization, the product not of consumer sovereignty, as the Bush administration suggested, but of the vast corporate power of the oil-automobile nexus.

To what lengths will this addiction be pursued? The answer is not simply to the ends of the earth; the mad pursuit has also taken us to the bottom of the ocean. Deepwater exploration is the latest holy grail of Big Oil. On August 2, 2007, a Russian submarine with two parliamentarians on board planted a titanium flag two miles beneath the North Pole. At stake were lucrative new oil and gas fields—by some estimates ten billion tons of oil—on the Arctic sea floor. Two weeks later, it was announced that the fabled Northwest Passage was navigable for the first time in recorded history, facilitating the new oil frontier. The ecological preconditions for this unprecedented event were, of course, global warming—another product of Big Oil.

In late 2006, a consortium discovered oil at a staggering depth in the Gulf of Mexico. The test well, Jack-2, delved through 7,000 feet of water and 20,000 feet of sea floor to tap oil trapped in tertiary rock laid down 60 million years ago. The drill ships and production platforms required to undertake such deep drilling are massive floating structures, much larger than the largest aircraft carriers and costing well over a half billion dollars (and close to a

Above:
IN THE OGONILAND VILLAGE of Kpean, an oil wellhead that was leaking for weeks turns into a raging inferno.

Left:
IN THE OIL TOWN of Afiesere in the Niger Delta, a Urohobo woman uses the heat of a controlled gas flare to bake *krokpo-garri* (tapioca).

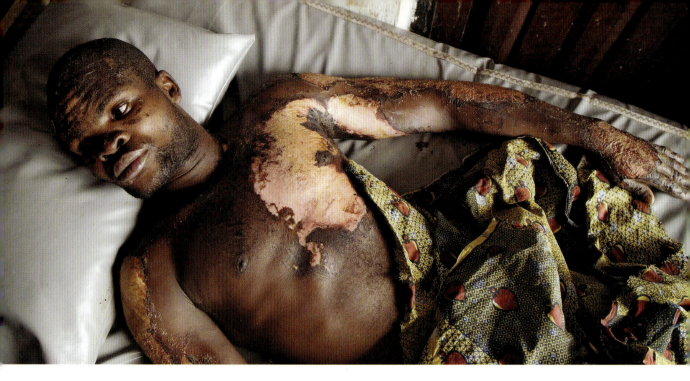

Clockwise from above:

PATRICK OGHOGHO, a laborer from Bayelsa State, suffered third- and fourth-degree burns when Nigerian soldiers attacked and burned down Aker Base, a Port Harcourt slum. This was apparently in reprisal for the killing of an army sergeant during the kidnapping of a foreign oil worker.

STUDENTS in a run-down primary school in Ogulagha take their exams. Teachers often do not show up because they are paid irregularly.

A RESIDENT of Aker Base, a Port Harcourt slum, picks through the remains of her house after the Nigerian military destroyed the neighborhood.

million dollars a day to rent). In 2007, the vast new Tupi field in Brazilian coastal waters was discovered in 200 meters of water below a massive layer of salt in hugely inhospitable geological conditions. One test well cost more than $250 million to drill. But the addict, says Burroughs, knows no limits to satiate his craving.

The deadly logic of addiction—the drive to acquire oil at all costs—is experienced with particular ferocity in the oil-producing states of the equatorial region and global south. Ed Kashi's work in the Niger Delta documents the existential nightmare of what oil wealth means in reality. An inventory of the by-products of Nigerian oil production is a salutary, if dismal, exercise: 85 percent of Nigerian oil revenues accrue to 1 percent of the population. According to former World Bank president Paul Wolfowitz, at least $100 billion of the $600 billion in oil revenues collected since 1960 have simply "gone missing." Nigerian anti-corruption czar Nuhu Ribadu says that 70 percent of the country's oil wealth has been stolen or wasted. From 1965 to 2004 Nigeria's per-capita income actually fell from $250 to $212, while income distribution deteriorated markedly. Between 1970 and 2000, the percentage of people subsisting on less than one dollar a day in Nigeria grew from 36 percent to more than 70 percent, from 19 million to a staggering 90 million. During the last decade of Croesian oil riches, GDP per capita and life expectancy in Nigeria have, according to World

TRANS AMADI SLAUGHTER is the largest slaughterhouse in the Niger Delta. Workers kill thousands of animals a day, roast them over burning tires and prepare the meat for sale throughout the delta. Fish was traditionally the main source of protein here, but fish stocks have dwindled due to overfishing and oil pollution.

Left and right, above:
IN THE IGAW VILLAGE of
Oporoza, Movement for the
Emancipation of the Niger
Delta (MEND) fighters attend
a funeral for colleagues killed
in a Nigerian army ambush.
MEND was returning a Shell
worker they took hostage
when Nigerian military boats
ambushed them, killing the
hostage and nine guerrillas.

Bank estimates, both fallen. To conclude, as the International Monetary Fund has, Nigeria's $600 billion in oil revenue has actually contributed to a *decline* in the country's standard of living. No wonder former Venezuelan oil minister and OPEC cofounder Juan Pablo Perez Alfonzo dubbed oil "the devil's excrement."

Perez proved prophetic. After nearly four decades of oil riches, Venezuela's per-capita income is lower than it was in 1960. But nowhere is the so-called resource curse more profound and visible than across the Niger Delta oil fields. For the vast majority of the delta's 30 million people, oil has brought only misery, violence, economic and cultural degradation, and a dying ecosystem. A United Nations report on human development in the delta concluded, "The vast resources from an international industry have barely touched pervasive local poverty." By conservative oil-industry estimates there were almost 7,000 oil spills between 1970 and 2000, more than one each day (the real figure might be twice or three times that number). Gas flaring (burning off natural gas released by oil drilling) in the delta produces 70 million metric tons of carbon emissions a year—"a substantial proportion of worldwide greenhouse gas," according to the World Bank. A World Wildlife Fund report released in 2006 simply referred to the Niger

Delta as one of the most polluted places on the face of the earth.

By almost any measure, Nigeria's oil-producing states are a calamity. The United Nations estimates that between 1996 and 2002, the human development indices (education, life expectancy, income) actually *fell* in the core oil-producing states. Since 2000, the rage felt by marginalized and unemployed men across the Niger Delta has taken a militant turn. In late 2005 an armed insurgency erupted in the creeks of the Delta, led by the Movement for the Emancipation of the Niger Delta (MEND). For the better part of two years, the Niger Delta has been more or less ungovernable—effectively a war zone.

The history of our addiction to oil is a chronicle of violence, corruption and the worst excesses of frontier capitalism and social Darwinism. It was the case when the Nobel and Rothschild families grappled for control of Caspian Sea oil in the late nineteenth century; it is just as true now in the Gulf of Guinea. Like crack, tobacco or any other addiction enabled by a vast, powerful industry (Is it surprising that Big Tobacco financially supported global warming skeptics for years?), our oil addiction is hugely destructive, defies logic and is nearly impossible to break. But unlike crack and tobacco, we will eventually run out of oil.

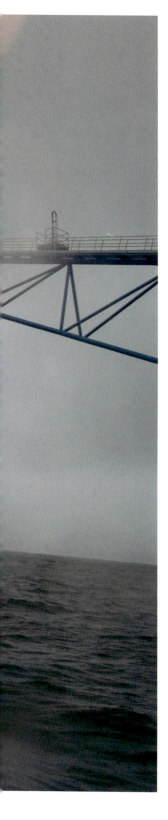

ED KASHI

Ed Kashi (US) has photographed in more than sixty countries. His images have appeared in *The New York Times Magazine, Time, Geo, Newsweek* and many other publications. He shot eleven major stories for *National Geographic*. His first *Geographic* cover story was published as the book *When the Borders Bleed: The Struggle of the Kurds*. His project on Protestants in Northern Ireland was published as *The Protestants: No Surrender*. His work on West Bank Jewish settlers received a World Press Photo award. In 2003 he completed an eight-year project, *Aging in America: The Years Ahead*, that included an exhibit, award-winning documentary film, Web site and book. The project won prizes from Pictures of the Year and World Press Photo. Kashi and his wife, writer/filmmaker Julie Winokur, founded Talking Eyes Media, a multimedia nonprofit that produced a book and exhibition called *Denied: The Crisis of America's Uninsured*.

THE OIL RIG Auntie Julie the Martyr, operated by Conoil, off the coast of Sanghana town in the Niger Delta.

MICHAEL WATTS

Michael Watts (UK) is Chancellor's Professor of Geography and Development Studies and director of the Center for African Studies at the University of California, Berkeley. He has held visiting appointments at the Museum of Natural History and the National Science Foundation. Watts has received grants from the Rockefeller, MacArthur and Guggenheim Foundations, the last to study the interplay of oil, politics and wealth in West Africa. He is the author of five books and the Geopolitics article "Resource Curse? Governmentality, Oil and Power in the Niger Delta." His latest book, in cooperation with photographer Ed Kashi, is titled *Curse of the Black Gold: 50 Years of Oil in the Niger Delta*.

THE GREATEST MIGRATION

The Third World Moves to the City

I WAS FOURTEEN YEARS OLD when I discovered what it was like inside a squatter settlement. Oliver, one of the bookkeepers who worked in my father's office in downtown Lagos, Nigeria, invited me to his home on the northwestern shores of Lagos Island.

It shocked me at the time that Oliver, scrupulously turned out every day in a freshly laundered white shirt and neatly pressed trousers like all of his colleagues, lived in a two-room shack with earthen floors and a tin roof, part of a makeshift compound of dwellings, one of many interconnected by narrow lanes and interlaced with open drainage ditches that did double duty as sewers. Oliver had come to Lagos from the (then) small town of Abeokuta, looking for a job commensurate to his schooling, something that would support his young family. He found the job, but he couldn't find any accommodations he could afford, so, like tens of millions of other ambitious young men from the countryside, he moved into a squat.

That was almost fifty years ago, placing Oliver in the vanguard of the Great Rural-Urban Migration, the mass movement of

JAKARTA, INDONESIA'S WEALTH is in the hands of a privileged minority, while most people struggle in poor, polluted slums.

by **PAUL KNOX**

photographs by **SEBASTIÃO SALGADO**

About half of the world's population now lives in cities, and of those 3.3 billion people, at least one billion are squatters.

people around the globe from rural regions and small towns to big cities in search of economic and political security in an increasingly turbulent and economically unforgiving world. It is difficult to say just how many have taken part in the great migration. In many parts of the world, urban growth is taking place at such a pace and under such chaotic conditions that experts can provide only informed estimates. It is generally agreed, however, that about half of the world's population now lives in cities; and that of those 3.3 billion or so people, at least 1 billion are squatters. To put these figures in perspective: Only 30 percent of the world's population was urbanized in 1950; there were only 83 metropolitan areas of a million or more people, and only eight metropolitan areas of five million or more. There are now approximately 400 metropolitan areas of a million or more people, 80 percent with more than five million inhabitants. Projections for 2015 suggest that there will be around 540 cities with a population of a million or more including roughly 60 cities of five million or more. And the migration shows no sign of abating. Every day, nearly 200,000 mostly Third World people move to big cities—the equivalent of two Tokyos a year.

The Great Rural-Urban Migration has consisted of more than a billion people like Oliver, squeezed from rural areas that can no longer provide a living to growing populations, plus refugees from civil wars, oppression and environmental disasters such as deforestation, overgrazing, drought and flooding. These mostly economic refugees are pushed into big cities by the hope, albeit slim and often illusory, of somehow gaining access to schools, health clinics, piped water and the kinds of public facilities and services that are typically unavailable in the rural regions of less-developed countries. A small fraction of immigrants with qualifications—like Oliver—have a realistic chance of finding a job. But for all rural immigrants, cities retain the venerable lure of modernization and the appeal of consumer goods—attractions that are now directly beamed into rural areas via satellite television. The resultant migration streams are comprised disproportionately of teenagers and young adults, who bring exceptionally high rates of natural population increase to their destination cities.

The result is that big cities throughout the less-developed regions of the world have rapidly become mega-cities of 5, 10 or 20 million inhabitants. Cairo, Dhaka, Jakarta, Karachi, Lagos, Manila, Mexico City, São Paulo and the Indian cities of Delhi, Kolkata and Mumbai are the exemplars, mega-cities whose singular characteristic, apart from sheer size, is that millions of their inhabitants—typically well over one-third and sometimes up to three-quarters of their total population—live in makeshift squatter settlements. In Nairobi, Kenya, 1.5 million people—40 percent of the metropolitan-area population—live in such settlements. In Mumbai, the dynamic metropolis that accounts for 40 percent of the tax revenues of the entire country of India, more than six million people—about half of the total population—live in squatter housing. The residents of these squatter settlements are ordinary people with skills, families, lives, possessions, hopes and dreams. They are laborers, gardeners, bookkeepers, drivers, maids, entrepreneurs and civil servants; they are the unregistered workforce of informal economies in which "work" means anything that ensures

SEEKING A BETTER LIFE
in Europe, North African immigrants land at night in Gibraltar, Spain.

survival: shining shoes, guiding cars into parking spaces, chasing street kids away from outdoor cafés, sewing, making fireworks. And they are the unemployed, the underemployed and petty criminals.

What they have in common are incomes that offer them no chance of ever affording a place within the formal housing markets of cities that simply cannot cope with the pace and scale of population growth. So they squat, building homes illegally on unoccupied land simply because they can't afford any other place to live. Beginning with scavenged materials—offcuts of wood, leftover cardboard, plastic sheeting, planks, tarpaper, corrugated iron, and discarded doors and window frames—they aspire to upgrade later to brick, cinderblock or clay tiles as opportunities present themselves.

But because the massive squatter settlements yield no tax revenues, there are limited municipal funds for providing adequate health and educational services or for maintaining anything resembling a clean, safe environment. Squatter housing is typically built in the least desirable urban locations: derelict sites, poorly drained land prone to flooding, steep slopes prone to mudslides, even cemeteries and waste dumps. Open sewers are common; basic services such as electricity, running water, garbage collection, lighting and security are rare. In the absence of any municipal entity willing to fund or organize the essentials of urban infrastructure, squatter neighborhoods are marginal, life-threatening settings, their residents trapped in the conditions so powerfully documented, over the course of years, in Jakarta, Shanghai, São Paulo, Mexico City and Mumbai by Sebastião Salgado's photographs.

Water supply is an acute problem for many squatter communities, so much so that residents must wait in long lines to fill even one bucket of water because communal taps often function for only a few hours every day. Street vendors, who get their water from private tanker and borehole operators, sell water from two- or four-gallon cans and typically charge five to ten times the local rate set by public water utilities; in some places they charge fifty to a hundred times as much. So once again, it costs more to be poor.

In many cities, less than one-third of all garbage and solid waste is collected and removed. The rest is partially recycled informally

Squatter housing is typically built in the least desirable urban locations: derelict sites, poorly drained land prone to flooding, steep slopes prone to mudslides, even cemeteries and waste dumps.

Top and bottom:
AT THE RODOVIÁRIO DE TIETÊ bus terminal in São Paulo, a young woman in her best attire has just arrived from the countryside. With a metropolitan population of more than 20 million people (up from 16 million in 1996), São Paulo is a powerful magnet for peasant migrants.

or tipped into gullies, canals or rivers, or simply left to rot. Mounds of garbage seep rancid juices onto sidewalks and into homes; industrial and human wastes pile up in lakes and lagoons and pollute long stretches of rivers, estuaries and coastal zones; chemicals leaching from uncontrolled dump sites pollute groundwater. And without effective regulation, tons of lead, sulfur oxides, fluorides, carbon monoxide, nitrogen oxides and petrochemical oxidants are pumped into the atmosphere every day, adding to air pollution caused by the burning of charcoal, wood and kerosene for fuel and cooking. The results are predictable. At least 600 million urban poor, mostly squatters, live in settings where malaria, gastroenteritis, conjunctivitis, diarrhea, respiratory infections and tuberculosis are endemic; children brought up in these environments are fifty times as likely to die before the age of five as those born in affluent countries. Worldwide, ten million people each year meet an early death as a result of living in such conditions. The statistics are numbing, while Salgado's photographs still shock.

Salgado's photographs also suggest that squatter settlements, although physically fragile and environmentally dangerous, can be socially and economically resilient. Given a degree of stability, with electricity and water supplies, squatter communities can develop a measure of ad-hoc consumerism along with their own social and economic structures and institutions: squatter builders and squatter contractors, squatter landlords and squatter tenants, squatter merchants and squatter consumers, squatter bars and squatter sidewalk cafes. Sultanbeyli, on the periphery of Istanbul, a former squatter suburb with some 200,000 inhabitants, famously created over time its own city hall, planning department, public works department, post office, sanitation department and bus service.

The Sultanbeyli example underlines the fact that migration and urbanization are not the problem: it's the speed of urban growth that's the immediate problem, combined with the incapacity to deal with it. But behind that incapacity is another, more intractable problem: the structural inequality of the global economic system, a legacy of the initial advantage established by more developed countries and a theme that has informed Salgado's work from the beginning.

It is important to remember that the industrialized regions of Britain, Europe and America experienced their own great rural-urban migration 150 years ago. The industrial era ushered in better diets, medical science and public health legislation that sharply lowered death rates and prompted a population explosion that in turn accelerated mass migrations to the industrial cities. As a result, conditions in the newly industrial cities of nineteenth-century Europe and America were just as shocking then as conditions in Third World mega-cities are now. Immigrant photographer Jacob Riis documented the squalid nineteenth-century slums of New York with the same intensity that Salgado now directs toward twenty-first-century Mumbai and Jakarta. But while they could not always cope with the influx, European and American industrial cities were hungry for labor, and there were at least the safety valves of emigration to other parts of the Americas, South Africa, Australia, and New Zealand.

Thanks largely to a combination of colonialism and imperialism, the cities of the developed world were able, in the long run, to secure and maintain their initial economic advantage (although they are now challenged by the mega-cities of China). In more recent decades, the structural inequality of an increasingly globalized world economy has been buttressed and sustained by a combination of neocolonialism, the global reach of transnational corporations, the commodity chains of monoculture agribusiness (growing one commodity crop to the exclusion of all others), the strategic priorities of neoconservative geopolitics and policies of economic shock therapy imposed in the course of misguided neoliberal market reforms.

When scientific medicine, better diets and public health improvements began to trigger population explosions in less-developed countries several decades ago, they simply could not follow the historical experience of developed countries. Their cities, potential engines of economic growth, were for the most part restricted by their subaltern relation to the global cities and manufacturing regions of North America, western Europe and Japan. Starved of capital and swamped by unskilled labor, they developed dual economies: a formal sector interfacing with the

*C*onditions in the newly industrial cities of nineteenth-century Europe and America were as shocking then as conditions in Third World mega-cities are now.

global economy and an informal sector driven by migrants' need
for survival.

Once the slums and squatter settlements were established, the
mega-cities of the less-developed world found that they couldn't
do without them. The informal sector provides a huge range of
cheap goods and services that reduce the cost of living for employ-
ees in the formal sector, allowing employers to keep wages low.
Industries in the formal sector rely on the fact that labor standards
in the informal sector are nearly impossible to enforce, so many
companies farm out their production using subcontracting schemes
that depend on unregistered men, women and children working
from their own homes in squatter settlements.

Thus, in contrast to the world's developed regions, where
urbanization largely resulted from economic growth, the urbanization of less-developed countries has been a consequence of demo-
graphic growth that preceded economic development. Rural
migrants have poured into cities out of desperation and hope rather
than being drawn by jobs and opportunities. Huge increases in
population took place well in advance of any significant levels of
industrialization or rural economic development. The result, for
the mainly rural populations of less-developed countries, was more
and more of worse and worse. Fast-growing rural populations suddenly faced an apparently hopeless future of drudgery and poverty.
As the more affluent core countries put up stronger barriers to
immigration, the only places left to turn to were the cities. Overall,
the metropolises of the less-developed countries have absorbed
four out of five of the 1.2 billion city dwellers added to the world's
population since 1970.

Salgado's haunting photographs are witness to a continuing
cycle of underdevelopment, migration and urban poverty in the
less-developed world. At the turn of the twentieth century, Jacob
Riis' photographs directly inspired the city fathers of New York to
stop blaming the poor for their poverty, close "police poorhouses"
and, finally, to direct resources toward alleviating the misery of the
city's slums. Although the problem is exponentially larger and far
more global at the turn of the twenty-first century, we can only
hope that Salgado's photographs may have the same effect.

SEBASTIÃO SALGADO

Sebastião Salgado (Brazil) decided to become a photojournalist while visiting Africa as an economist in the early seventies. Since then he has gained international acclaim for his large-scale photographic projects, including *Workers*, a study of manual labor around the world; *Migrations: Humanity in Transition*; and *The End of Polio*. Arguably the world's greatest living photojournalist, Salgado's more than fifty awards include the International Center of Photography's Photojournalist of the Year prize, the Eugene Smith Award for Humanitarian Photography and the Alfred Eisenstaedt Life Legend Award.

PAUL KNOX

Paul Knox (UK) is University Distinguished Professor and Senior Fellow for International Advancement at Virginia Tech. From 1997 to 2006, he was dean of Virginia Tech's College of Architecture and Urban Studies. Knox is an expert in urban and regional development theory and comparative urbanization. He serves on the editorial board of seven international journals and was coeditor of the *Journal of Urban Affairs*. His award-winning books and textbooks include *World Regions in Global Context: Peoples, Places, and Environments*; *Human Geography*; *Urbanization: An Introduction to Urban Geography*; *Urban Social Geography*; and *The Geography of the World Economy*. He is currently writing *Metroburbia, USA*.

CHURCH GATE is the terminus of the Western Railroad line, which brings 2.7 million commuters into Mumbai every day.

THE FENCE

Deconstructing America's "Immigration Crisis"

IN TIJUANA, on the Mexican side of the border, the fence is covered with hundreds of memorials to those who died trying to cross into the United States.

DESPITE ALL THE HYPE AND HYSTERIA, the flow of migrants between Mexico and the United States is neither new nor unusual. Mexican migrants have been crossing the border in large numbers since 1907. What has varied over time is not the number of Mexicans entering the United States, but rather how government officials and the American public have greeted their arrival. Basically, whenever the United States needs additional workers, as we did during World War I, World War II, and several economic booms, Mexican migrants have been welcome. When there is an economic bust or a security issue, America slams the door.

Over the last century, US policy toward Mexican immigration has ranged from active recruitment to passive acceptance to mass deportation—and, most recently, a senseless attempt to somehow fence off a 1,969-mile-long border. But these many radical shifts in US policy have had less influence on the rate of entry than on the rate of

by **DOUGLAS S. MASSEY**
photographs by **ANTHONY SUAU**

Officials cordoned off Mexican neighborhoods and systematically arrested anyone who could not prove, on the spot, that they had the legal right to be in the United States.

Top:
IN DOUGLAS, ARIZONA, a ranch owner who lives on a section of the border where thousands of illegal immigrants cross each year has placed this warning sign in his field.

Bottom and following pages:
THE US NATIONAL GUARD constructs a new section of border fence near the San Luis port of entry. The fence is partially buried to keep illegal immigrants from digging under it.

departure, the place of crossing, the location of settlement and the legal status of the people involved. Although the current border situation can be fairly described as an immigration crisis, it stems from a series of unintended consequences and is essentially a crisis of our own making. As usual, it helps to understand the history.

Mass migration from Mexico began in 1907, when Japan and the United States reached an understanding called the Gentlemen's Agreement. Officials in Japan agreed to prevent their citizens from leaving for the United States, and in return, American officials agreed not to prohibit them from entering. As this agreement took effect, labor shortages emerged throughout the American West, leading employers to recruit workers from south of the border. Mexican immigration grew steadily through 1914 and then surged with the onset of World War I. Once America entered the conflict, the US government organized a formal temporary worker program.

When the war ended, nativist forces in the United States passed a series of quota laws that sharply reduced immigration from southern and eastern Europe, heretofore the largest source of immigrants. The new restrictions on European immigration, combined with a decade-long economic boom known as the Roaring Twenties, caused severe labor shortages that were increasingly filled by Mexicans; the immigration quotas did not apply to nations in the Western Hemisphere, leaving Mexicans free to enter the United States in large numbers. During the 1920s, legal immigration from Mexico to the United States reached heights not equaled before or since.

With the crash of the stock market in 1929 and the onset of the Great Depression, two decades of active public and private recruitment came to an abrupt halt. In the context of rising unemployment and growing demands for public relief, i.e., "welfare," Mexican immigrants were tautologically portrayed as both taking American jobs and receiving welfare benefits that belonged to "real" Americans. In response, federal authorities organized a massive deportation campaign. State and local officials cordoned off Mexican neighborhoods and systematically swept through, arresting anyone who could not prove, on the spot, that they had the legal right to be in the United States. From 1929 to 1939 some

**IN CALEXICO,
CALIFORNIA,** the National
Guard monitors cameras
placed in towers along the
border. Most of the border is
under camera surveillance.

470,000 Mexicans, including many US citizens and legal residents, were arrested and forcibly removed from the United States without due process.

By the end of the decade, the flood tide of the 1920s was reduced to a trickle and mass Mexican immigration was effectively dead, at least for the moment. However, as fast as the welcome mat had been withdrawn in 1929, it was put back in place once the United States was drawn into World War II. In 1942, authorities in Washington approached their counterparts in Mexico City and negotiated a bilateral agreement known as the Bracero Accord, which arranged for the recruitment and importation of temporary agricultural workers. The Bracero Program grew throughout the war, and by 1945 some 170,000 Mexicans had come and gone as temporary workers.

The US economy boomed after the war ended, and native US workers never really returned to agriculture. Despite the pleas of growers, Congress steadfastly refused to authorize any expansion of the Bracero Program; in response, employers took matters into

their own hands and began to recruit Mexicans outside of official channels, thereby beginning a new stream of illegal or undocumented migration. By the early 1950s, the annual number of undocumented workers greatly exceeded the annual count of braceros. A brief recession followed the end of the Korean War and coincided with an upsurge in anti-foreigner hysteria under McCarthyism; in 1953, illegal migration became a divisive political issue, with Mexicans framed as invaders and infiltrators who threatened the nation's culture and values.

US officials responded to this "crisis" with a two-pronged strategy. On the one hand, with great public fanfare, the US Border Patrol launched "Operation Wetback" to militarize the border and raid farms throughout the Southwest. By 1954, the number of Mexicans apprehended by Border Patrol agents reached one million for the first time in history. On the other hand, quietly and with much less fanfare, Congress more than doubled the size of the Bracero Program to around 440,000 workers per year. This expansion finally met the demand for farm labor, and apprehensions

IN 2007, the US National Guard placed miles of vehicle barriers along a stretch of open desert west of Calexico. The barrier blocks what was once an open road for smugglers, who simply drove vehicles loaded with drugs into the United States.

IN AGUA PRIETA, a young
Mexican man and woman
jump the border fence just
after dawn.

IN THE LECHERÍA train yards near Mexico City, Central Americans jump northbound trains headed toward the border. Stories abound of those killed when they fell from trains or were beaten and robbed by Mexican authorities.

dropped from a million in 1954 to just 30,000 in 1959. The border crisis had been resolved, not by police actions at the border but by the quiet expansion of guest worker migration. The volume of Mexican immigration continued much as before, only now the migrants were guest workers.

The Bracero Program came undone in the context of the burgeoning civil rights movement of the 1960s, which viewed the program as an exploitive labor system on a par with Southern sharecropping. Congress began to phase out the program in 1960 and terminated it entirely in 1964. Growers responded by sponsoring former braceros as legal permanent residents, leading to an increase in legal immigration. In 1965, however, Congress passed reform legislation that ended the restrictive quotas on immigration from Asia, Africa and parts of Europe, replacing them with a neutral system that gave 20,000 visas to each nation. And although the provisions were little noticed at the time, the 1965 amendments also instituted the first-ever numerical limitations on immigration from the Western Hemisphere, capping it at 120,000 persons per year.

The new system took effect in 1968 and opened up new flows from countries that heretofore had not sent many immigrants to American shores, most notably the nations of Asia. The conditions responsible for mass emigration from Europe before 1920 had largely disappeared by the 1960s, however, so European immigration did not revive. Despite the hemispheric quota, legal immigration from Mexico continued to rise until 1976, when Congress imposed the

I f the United States had intentionally set out to design a dysfunctional immigration system, it could hardly have done a better job.

per-country limit of 20,000 annual visas on nations in the Western Hemisphere. In the years since 1960, Mexico had gone from annual access to 440,000 temporary visas and an unlimited number of resident visas to zero temporary visas and just 20,000 resident visas.

This sudden curtailment of visas quickly and predictably yielded a rising tide of undocumented migration. Annual apprehensions of Mexicans at the border climbed steadily to 1.3 million in 1985. The early 1980s yielded another economic recession that coincided with a resurgence of anti-communist hysteria as Ronald Reagan escalated the Cold War through proxy confrontations in Latin America. Reagan was the first president to declare undocumented immigration a threat to national security. He warned Americans about "a tidal wave of refugees" from communist aggression and, referring to the unpopular wave of Cuban refugees under President Carter, he said, "this time they'll be 'feet people' and not boat people."

In this context of economic fear and ideological hysteria, Congress in 1986 passed the Immigration Reform and Control Act. In the same year, Mexican leaders finally succumbed to pressure from Washington and agreed to open Mexico's economy by joining the General Agreement on Tariffs and Trade. Since that fateful date, US policy toward Mexico has moved simultaneously in opposite directions, yielding a new politics of contradiction that has worked to the detriment of Mexico, the United States and the people who travel between them.

On the one hand, both countries by mutual agreement have taken concrete steps to integrate their economies. In 1994, the North American Free Trade Agreement (NAFTA) was enacted to reduce barriers to cross-border movements of goods, capital, information, services, natural resources and certain kinds of people. This produced an eight-fold increase in total trade in only six years. On the other hand, even as markets throughout North America moved headlong toward consolidation, US authorities tried to maintain separate labor markets by steadily militarizing the border. Since 1986, the Border Patrol's budget has increased ten times and the number of agents has tripled. The southern border of the United States is now the most fortified frontier between peaceful trading nations anywhere on earth.

The fruits of these contradictions have been tragic, and the dimension of the tragedy is compounded by the fact that US policy has been worse than useless; it has been counterproductive. At great cost to all, our attempt to have our cake and eat it too—that is, to integrate all markets except the labor market—has made the problems associated with immigration worse, not better. The militarization of the border in San Diego and El Paso has diverted migrants into remote Arizona deserts and wild sections of the Rio Grande, tripling the death rate among undocumented migrants and redirecting immigrants to new destinations throughout the United States. By shifting migrants into more remote sections of the border, moreover, US policy reduced the probability of apprehension from around 30 percent to around 10 percent while raising out-of-pocket expenses to migrants, who still come in approximately the same numbers. Migrants have quite logically responded by reducing their number of border crossings—not by forgoing migration altogether, but by hunkering down and staying longer once they get in. Although no one would know it from American media coverage, the rate of undocumented entry has not increased in twenty-five years. What has changed is the rate of undocumented exit, which has dropped by 50 percent.

The United States currently spends more than $5 billion per year on immigration enforcement. And in the end, it has only succeeded in transforming what was once a small, circular flow of male workers who temporarily settled in three states into a much larger national population of families that have settled in all fifty states. US immigration policy has thereby driven up the cost to American taxpayers, killed some 400 additional people per year on the border and reduced the rate of border apprehension to record lows. As a further result of these policies, the undocumented population has grown at an unprecedented rate and now numbers more than 12 million people. One-third of all Mexican immigrants in the United States are presently undocumented and vulnerable to the worst forms of exploitation and victimization. If the United States had intentionally set out to design a dysfunctional and immoral immigration system over the past two decades, it could hardly have done a better job.

Following pages,
clockwise from top left:
A SPECIAL OPERATIONS unit of the US Border Patrol apprehends a group of illegals.

IN NOGALES, ARIZONA, the Border Patrol detains four Mexicans who jumped the fence.

ONE OF TWO holding centers in Nogales set up to control and deport illegal immigrants.

ROUGHLY 30 MILES into the United States, piles of debris are scattered across a dry riverbed. Illegals smuggled to this spot, inaccessible by vehicle, are told to drop all unnecessary items before continuing to the main road.

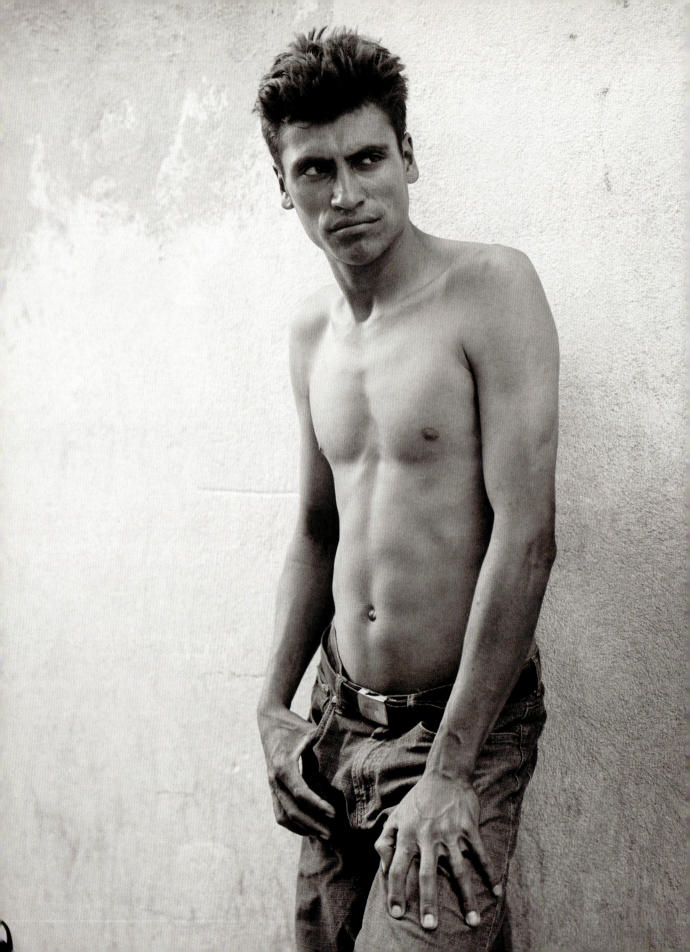

ANTHONY SUAU

Anthony Suau, an American living in Paris, won a Pulitzer Prize for his photographs of the 1984 famine in Ethiopia, the World Press Photo of the Year in 1987 for a photo taken during a demonstration in South Korea and the Robert Capa Gold Medal in 1995 for his photos from Chechnya. He has worked for *Time* magazine for many years and has published several books, including *Beyond the Fall*, a ten-year project portraying the transition of the Eastern Bloc after the fall of the Berlin Wall, and *Fear This*, about the war of images and slogans that play out at home while America is at war in Iraq.

DOUGLAS S. MASSEY

Douglas S. Massey (US) is the Henry G. Bryant Professor of Sociology and Public Affairs at Princeton University's Woodrow Wilson School of Public and International Affairs. He specializes in the sociology of immigration. Massey was president of the American Sociological Association and is currently president of the American Academy of Political and Social Science. His books include *Crossing the Border: Research from the Mexican Migration Project; Beyond Smoke and Mirrors: Mexican Immigration in an Era of Economic Integration; Worlds in Motion: International Migration at the End of the Millennium;* and *Return to Azatlan: The Social Process of International Migration from Western Mexico.*

AT CASA DEL MIGRANTE NAZARETH, a shelter in the border town of Nuevo Laredo, migrants such as Ramón Ernesto Rodríguez, 23, from Honduras, can receive up to three days of free food and shelter. The house is run by a Catholic priest, nuns and lay clergy from the small Church of Saint Joseph nearby.

INFECTED OR AFFECTED

Curing AIDS in Sub-Saharan Africa

WHEN HIV WAS FIRST IDENTIFIED IN 1983, many researchers thought it would be easy to develop a vaccine to protect people against it, but today that optimism is rapidly fading. To understand why HIV is such a powerful killer, it helps to know what happens when a person becomes infected.

A YOUNG AIDS VICTIM in a Lusaka, Zambia, morgue.

HIV is a spherical virus whose surface is covered with tiny stalks. There is a ball at the end of each stalk that functions like a key, enabling HIV to break into particular white blood cells—called CD4 cells—that help protect the body from disease. Once inside the CD4 cells, the virus hijacks the DNA-copying machinery and forces the cells to churn out millions of new viruses until the cells eventually burst open and disintegrate or clump together and die. In the bloodstream of HIV-positive people, a billion CD4 cells are hijacked and killed each day, and 100 billion new HIV viruses are produced.

Within a few weeks, the immune system begins making cells and antibodies that destroy most of the virus particles, but some of the 100 billion new viruses escape by mutating: they change

by **HELEN EPSTEIN**
photographs by **TOM STODDART**

slightly, infect new cells and continue to reproduce. The body must make new cells and antibodies to fight the mutants, but the mutants mutate again, necessitating yet another immune response. Soon the virus has embedded itself into so many CD4 cells that it is impossible for the immune system to clear it without destroying itself in the process. As the CD4 cells die off, the body loses its ability to respond to a range of other infections. The patient, slowly consumed by diseases that are harmless to other people, eventually dies.

In 1996, researchers showed that combinations of anti-retroviral drugs can relieve the symptoms and extend the lives of HIV-positive people, sometimes by decades. However, these drugs are not a cure; they don't work for everyone; and they can have severe side effects. They also don't stop the virus from spreading, because those most likely to spread the virus to others are often at an early stage of infection and are not in need of treatment. Treating AIDS patients in Africa, where two-thirds of all HIV-positive people now live, is particularly difficult because Africa's health-care infrastructure is in such a dire state. This means treatment programs are expensive and difficult to administer, even when the drugs are practically free. Those who do receive treatment can expect to gain, on average, only an extra six or seven years of life because the virus eventually develops resistance, necessitating second- and third-line treatment, currently all but unavailable in Africa. It is impossible to put a price on seven years of anyone's life, least of all that of an African mother whose children would otherwise be orphaned, but it would be better by far if that mother had never become infected in the first place.

To date, the closest thing to a vaccine to prevent HIV is male circumcision, which was shown in 2006 to reduce the risk of HIV transmission by roughly 65 percent. The widespread practice of male circumcision in the predominantly Muslim countries of West Africa may largely explain why the virus is much less common there than it is along the eastern and southern rim of the continent. Every man who is willing to undergo the procedure should have access to cheap, safe circumcision services. But it may take years to develop such services, and in the meantime, millions more people will be infected. Furthermore, even in West African cities

For now, our best weapon against the virus remains behavior change.

where nearly all men are circumcised, HIV infection rates are sometimes quite high.

For now, our best weapon against the virus remains behavior change. But health officials have been trying to get people to change their behavior since the epidemic emerged twenty-seven years ago, and the message seems to have fallen on deaf ears. What can be done?

One thing we can do is to explore what happened in places where the epidemic did turn around. I've been thinking about this for nearly fifteen years, and it's become increasingly clear to me that

JANET JOHN, 23,
sick from HIV, at home in Mwanza, Tanzania.

the key to fighting AIDS lies in something for which public health has no name or program. It is best described as a sense of solidarity, compassion and mutual support that is impossible to quantify or measure. It has to be this way. Because our sexuality is shaped by society, and because sex itself involves more than one person, behavior change is a collective act, not an individual act. That's why social mobilization is so important. And that's why HIV prevention is so difficult.

But sometimes it works. So far, the two clearest examples are seemingly very different from each other: the small East African nation of Uganda in the late 1980s and early 1990s, and gay men the world over a few years earlier. In both places there was a massive, collective shift in sexual norms—mainly reductions in sexual partners and increased condom use. It was so sudden that in retrospect it seemed like a phase transition in nature, as when ice turns to water or clouds condense to produce rain.

In both places, these shifts were abetted by extraordinary activism that involved people living with HIV, their families and their friends. Almost as soon as the first bulletins about a new disease affecting homosexual men appeared in US newspapers in 1981, the gay community rose up against it. They argued about bathhouses and condoms; they chained themselves to government buildings to protest official inaction; they nursed their dying friends. If you visit the AIDS section of any library, you'll find a wall of literature from that time: poems, plays, memoirs, art books, philosophical essays. It was like a mass conversation.

Something similar happened in Uganda that caused the HIV rate to plummet by about 70 percent during the 1990s. I was working in Uganda at that time, and I remember thinking that although the epidemic there was different from the gay epidemic worldwide, the response was remarkably similar. There were plays, vigils and marches, and everyone talked about AIDS in highly personal ways. There was vigorous public debate about condoms and about how men and women treated one another. Uganda had a vibrant women's movement, and AIDS fit right into their agenda too. Throughout the country, people volunteered to care for the sick and their orphaned children. Some of these caregivers were supported by donors and churches, but most simply volunteered. As one man who remembers this time explained to me: "You'd go over, take care of the kids, sweep the floor, just sit and talk to the patient; you couldn't just do nothing."

Elsewhere in Africa, the disease was shrouded in silence. When I visited KwaZulu-Natal—the South African province with the highest HIV infection rate—as recently as 2005, the hush surrounding the epidemic was so spooky that it surprised even me.

The Catholic Church had been running an AIDS treatment program at a local hospital for more than a year. Outreach teams set forth each day to care for sick people and encourage them to take HIV tests and, if necessary, join the treatment program. I spent a week following these caregivers on their rounds. As we went from one homestead to another and sat with dying patients and their families, no one, not once, said the word *AIDS*.

Patients told us they were suffering from ulcers or tuberculosis or pneumonia. AIDS orphans said their parents had been "bewitched" by a jealous neighbor. Many AIDS patients died in their houses, cared for with compassion but in silence, their condition shrouded in euphemisms.

Occasionally, I was told, HIV-positive men and women were thrown out of their houses, scorned by their relatives or quietly fired from their jobs when their status became known or even suspected.

"They all know it's AIDS, but they won't say it," one of the outreach workers told me. "And their families won't say it either. They think that if you have AIDS, you must be some kind of prostitute and have sex recklessly. That's why they deny it."

These attitudes are finally beginning to change, but it is worth asking what took so long. For a while, I've wondered whether it didn't have something to do with the fact that Ugandans—like gay men—knew where their risks came from, and this enabled a more open, compassionate, pragmatic response to the epidemic.

In 1986, long before rich donors such as the US government and the UN came on the scene, Ugandan health officials designed their own HIV prevention program. It was based on a crucial epidemiological insight that has, until recently, eluded most outsiders working on AIDS in Africa: the reason that HIV rates are high in

Because our sexuality is shaped by society, and because sex itself involves more than one person, behavior change is a collective act, not an individual act.

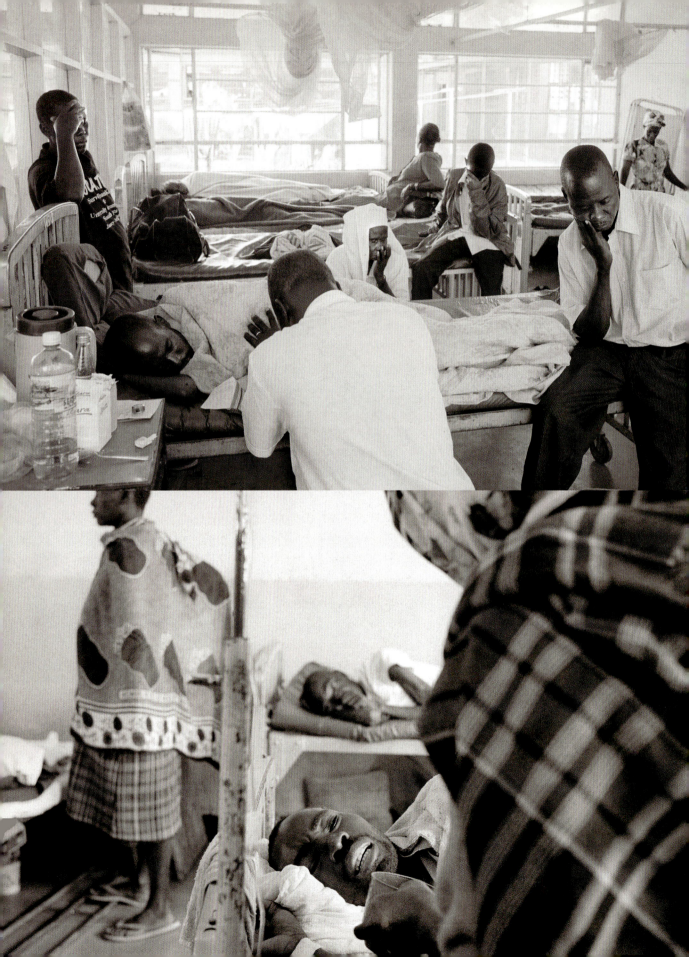

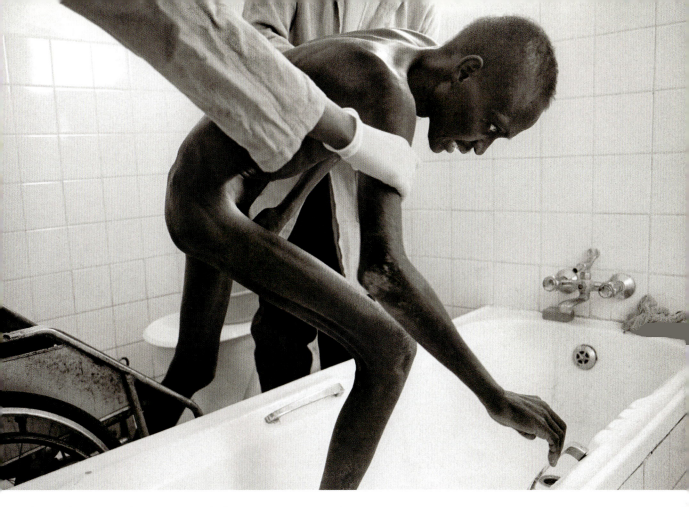

this region is not because people have so many sexual partners. In fact, most studies suggest that they have fewer partners, over a life-time, than Westerners. However, in many African societies, both men and women are more likely than people elsewhere to have more than one—perhaps two or three—overlapping long-term partnerships at the same time. This pattern of behavior differs from the serial monogamy more common in the West, and from the casual and commercial sexual encounters that occur everywhere. However, long-term concurrent relationships are far more danger-ous than serial monogamy because long-term, stable, interlocking relationships produce a virtual superhighway for HIV that puts everyone at risk—even faithful people, if their partners have con-current partners or did so in the past.

Thus, unlike in the rest of the world, where the virus is largely confined to "high-risk groups"—mainly prostitutes, intravenous-drug users and gay men—in East and Southern Africa everyone is at risk, from cabinet ministers to the women selling vegetables on

Clockwise from top left:
RELATIVES PRAY beside the bed of a dying man in Homa Bay District Hospital, Kenya. Eighty percent of admittees suffer from AIDS-related diseases.

KELVIN KALASHA, 30, is helped into his bath at the Mother of Mercy Hospice in Zambia.

A WOMAN offers food to her husband at Homa Bay District Hospital.

AIDS is neither an act of God nor a punishment for sin, but a terrible disease that no one deserves.

THE BODY of eight-year-old James Banda in a Zambian morgue.

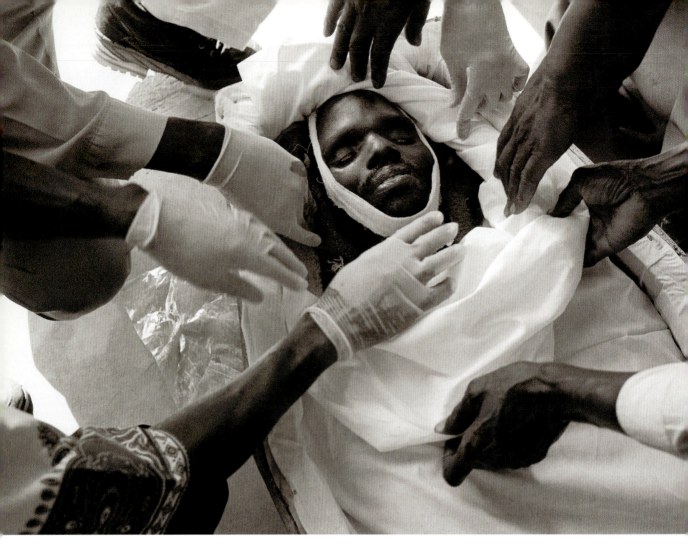

RELATIVES prepare an AIDS victim for burial in Zambia.

the street. Some of these people are men who support a wife and one long-term girlfriend. Others may be monogamous women whose partners have another partner or married women with a secret lover on the side. Very few are prostitutes or the types of people likely to frequent prostitutes, and most assume that because they have only one or a small number of partners they know well, they are safe. However, because of the network of concurrent partnerships, they are all on the HIV superhighway.

The Ugandans didn't use the term *concurrency*, but they did know that HIV was spreading through relatively ordinary families in relatively ordinary relationships and was not just a problem for prostitutes, truck drivers and other "immoral" people. "Don't point fingers" was a crucial message of those early campaigns.

To date, most AIDS campaigns elsewhere in Africa have promoted either condom use for "people at high risk," meaning pros-

titutes and their clients, or abstinence and faithfulness for everyone else. Across the continent, sexy billboards advertise the pleasures of condoms, and preachers give fire-and-brimstone sermons condemning adultery and sin. Obviously, neither approach is working very well. Moreover, by associating AIDS with "immoral" or "reckless" sexual behavior, these campaigns may exacerbate the stigma and denial associated with the disease, hindering treatment.

The HIV epidemic is finally beginning to subside in a number of African countries outside Uganda. As a result, a growing number of African men and women are raising their voices and talking about sex, gender relations and AIDS as never before. The courageous people in Tom Stoddart's photographs were the seed corn of that movement. Their dignified refusal to accept shame and denial is a powerful reminder that AIDS is neither an act of God nor a punishment for sin, but a terrible disease that no one deserves.

VILLAGERS carry the coffin of AIDS victim Damaresi Chilengwa for burial outside the village of Shakatwa, near Lusaka, Zambia.

Following pages:
THE FAMILY of Beauty Makwete mourns her death from AIDS, during her funeral at Mapepe Cemetery near Lusaka, Zambia.

A cross Africa, sexy billboards advertise the pleasures of condoms, and preachers give fire-and-brimstone sermons condemning adultery. Neither approach is working very well.

AT GOD'S POWER CHURCH in Nairobi, Kenya, a congregation prays for a cure for HIV/AIDS.

TOM STODDART

London-based Tom Stoddart (UK) has covered the Israeli invasion of Beirut, the fall of the Berlin Wall, the Greenpeace campaign to stop the slaughter of baby seals in Canada, and refugee crises in Sudan and Rwanda, among other stories. He won the Nikon Press Photographer of the Year award in 1990 and 1991. In August 1992 he was wounded while photographing war-torn Sarajevo for *The London Sunday Times*. More recently, Stoddart has been documenting the devastating effect of AIDS in sub-Saharan Africa. He contributed AIDS coverage to *A Day in the Life of Africa* (2002). His book *iWitness* (2004) chronicles nearly three decades of his work.

HELEN EPSTEIN

Helen Epstein (US) has written extensively about public health issues in developing countries and recently published the critically acclaimed book *The Invisible Cure: Africa, the West, and the Fight Against AIDS*. Her public health-related articles have been published in both academic journals and popular magazines such as *The New York Review of Books*, *The New York Times Magazine* and *Granta*. Epstein earned a PhD from Cambridge University and an MSc from the London School of Hygiene and Tropical Medicine. She was recently a visiting scholar at the Center for Health and Wellbeing at Princeton.

NEW COFFINS in Mjuli village, Malawi.

THE END OF MALARIA?

Rolling Back a Killer

TO REPEL MALARIAL mosquitoes, the Mora people of Amazonian Peru wear a natural insect repellent made from two fruits that stains the skin for several weeks.

IT SEEMS UNTHINKABLE THAT MALARIA, a disease carried by a fragile, seemingly insignificant mosquito, could be responsible for a global tragedy on the scale of 9/11…every single day. But it is true. Three thousand children—the equivalent of seven jumbo jets full of infants, toddlers and small children—die each day from malaria. This is an unacceptable reality that has only recently pulled at the heartstrings of the international community.

Malaria strikes the most vulnerable. Each year, 350 to 500 million malaria cases afflict primarily babies, children, pregnant women, people living in emergency situations and people with HIV/AIDS. Malaria is worst where poverty is greatest: in Africa, Latin America and Asia. It kills more children under five years old in Africa than in any other part of the world.

When malaria doesn't kill, it cripples and debilitates. Repeated malaria attacks can leave a child with neurological damage, severely impairing development. Poor families, especially mothers, then

by **AWA MARIE COLL-SECK**
photographs by **MAGGIE HALLAHAN**

By holding back economic and social development, malaria traps endemic countries in a vicious cycle of disease, poverty and death.

bear the burden of caring for these children for the rest of their lives, making the struggle for survival harder still. Pregnant women have reduced immunity, which makes them particularly susceptible to malarial infection and increases their risk of death and serious illnesses such as anemia.

The devastation doesn't stop there. Some estimate that malaria costs Africa $12 billion every year. By holding back economic and social development, malaria traps endemic countries in a vicious cycle of disease, poverty and death. It depletes the work force, discourages foreign investment and tourism, inhibits the development of internal trade, and adversely affects people's ability to pursue economic activities. This translates into lost GDP, lost productivity, and low economic growth.

Until only a few years ago, malaria was photographically depicted primarily in scientific magazines and medical journals: images of the distended, distraught body of a child comatose from a build-up of blood cells in the brain or super-magnified images of a mosquito's proboscis penetrating the unprotected flesh of a child too young to have any immunity, removing the child's blood and leaving in its place the deadly *Plasmodium falciparum* parasite. For all their power, these pictures described only the scientific search for solutions—the tools and medicines that could combat the disease. But they did not address the condition that nurtures the disease, namely poverty.

Maggie Hallahan's striking photographs shift that perspective, clearly demonstrating how malaria is both a cause and a consequence of poverty. We see communities caught up in a daily struggle with poverty; we see the individuals affected by malaria; but we also see glimpses of hope—the hard-won hope that arises when communities, and particularly women, are empowered with information and are provided access to the right medicines and insecticide-treated nets. And it's there that Maggie's pictures have captured the vital ingredient for success: any "end" to malaria will be achieved only if entire communities, particularly women, fully participate in the fight.

It was not that long ago that the world practically forgot about malaria, which was eradicated in Europe and America by the late

CONSOLATA VALEPUNSE,
a young Maasai woman
from northeastern Tanzania,
starts her first paying job at
the new Olyset mosquito net
factory in Arusha, Tanzania.

1950s. But several key events prodded our memory, and in recent years, the fight to roll back malaria has been joined with unprecedented vigor. One triggering event was the gathering of forty-four heads of state, along with international partners, in Abuja, Nigeria, in 2000. There, Africans . . . in Africa . . . made the necessary political commitment to escalate the battle against this ancient, neglected disease. Another critical step was the establishment of the Global Fund, a new international financing body set up to fight the unholy trinity of HIV/AIDS, tuberculosis and malaria. The establishment of the Global Fund—and its decision, prodded by the Roll Back Malaria Partnership, to designate and include malaria as "a disease of poverty"—signaled the advent of a new movement, and many international agencies, donors and private-sector partners drew together under the Global Fund umbrella.

Soon, new and more efficacious treatments were put in place, and the drug resistance that threatened older treatments, such as chloroquine, was held at bay. Innovative and highly effective insecticide-treated nets were introduced, and their production scaled upward as Global Fund grants helped finance national malaria eradication programs. By 2005 and 2006, Africa, Asia and Latin America were rolling out insecticide-treated nets by the millions, and countries such as Zambia, Togo, Niger, Gambia, Malawi, Kenya, Senegal and Guinea Bissau could cover 40 to 60 percent of their at-risk populations.

Just as important were new initiatives launched by established players. Twenty-three national airlines introduced a health levy that helps fund malaria treatments. The US government and the World Bank invested huge sums in new antimalaria programs. The G8 nations prioritized Africa, putting malaria and poverty firmly on the world agenda. And private philanthropists joined the fight. In 2007, the Bill and Melinda Gates Foundation, huge supporters of malaria research and development, raised the advocacy bar by boldly setting eradication as the long-term target for the global antimalaria community.

By 2008 we could speak in terms of a billion-dollar annual budget to fight malaria, tens of millions of nets distributed around the world, most malarial countries promoting effective treatments,

Africans . . . in Africa . . . made the necessary political commitment to escalate the battle against this ancient, neglected disease.

HELENA LEAH OLIMBAU nurses her boy, Edward Leisa, under a long-lasting insecticide-treated Olyset mosquito net in a rural Maasai village near Arusha, eastern Tanzania.

and many reintroducing systematic insecticide spraying indoors. Malaria partners are also devising ways to dramatically reduce the cost of treatments and make them more accessible. We still have a long way to go to put eradication firmly within our sight, but we should not underestimate these achievements. There is now a sense of possibility.

But Hallahan's photographs reveal one glaring gap yet to be sufficiently addressed—the urgent need for a higher level of investment in the people who actually live with malaria every day. The mother's lack of information, the abiding myths about the disease, the unrecognized and unmet needs of marginalized communities, and the terrible burden malaria places on women and girls all remind us that our progress is meaningful only when we can make a difference in the daily lives of every malaria victim.

Women bear the greatest responsibility for caring for these victims, yet in most endemic countries women have limited access to information, little decision-making power, and few financial resources, all of which would facilitate effective disease prevention and treatment at the community level.

The situation was not dissimilar to the days, many years ago, when I was a young doctor in Senegal. Then, as today, millions of poor women lived far from health centers and lacked basic health information. They had little access to either prevention measures or treatment. If their child was sick, they often had to seek permission from their husband—and then somehow raise the money—to transport the child to the nearest health worker or referral center. In many instances, mothers had to make the hard choice between buying medicine for one sick child and buying food for the rest of the family.

Many women didn't really understand why their child had become sick with fever in the first place—what had caused the illness, or how they could prevent or treat it. More often than not they would first take a sick child to a traditional healer, who would prescribe a mixture of herbs or potions, or evoke cleansing rituals to rid the child of the convulsions associated with cerebral malaria. The healers attributed these convulsions to "evil curses." While in Tanzania recently, I watched children act out the role of the traditional healer in a school play, demonstrating the role these healers still have in treating malaria in rural areas. As influential figures in the community, they need to be part of the solution, not part of the problem.

In many communities today, people still don't understand the causes and treatment of malaria. This is especially true of young mothers who drop out of school. They must be empowered with information and skills to protect themselves and their children, and they must be given the authority and economic ability to take their family's health into their own hands. Some potential solutions to this problem already exist. For example, small rural bank schemes that combine credit with health education have been successfully introduced on a limited scale. These programs simultaneously teach women how to care for their families and how to strengthen their income-generating ability. The biological and social factors that account for the different impact malaria has on women and men must be integrated into malaria control programs, and sound communication of behavioral change strategies must be prominently featured in all malaria education programs.

Furthermore, every family at risk must have at least one insecticide-treated net. There is good news in this area. Massive nationwide campaigns that combine immunization with net distribution have dramatically increased coverage in Africa. Maggie Hallahan's photograph of women standing in line in Madagascar could also have been taken in Mali, Niger, Benin or Togo. These women's stoic determination and patience are at once inspirational and heartrending. Many of them travel up to eight hours to reach the distribution point; then wait another five hours under a blazing sun, without shade or water, to receive an insecticide-treated net for their children's bed (and a measles vaccine for the children). After that, they must make the long journey home. But that arduous journey will pay off; these nets will save lives.

Getting nets into every home is only part of the solution, however. Making effective malaria medicines readily available at affordable prices, both in the city and in the countryside, is also necessary. This calls for distribution strategies that target everyone at risk and leave no one behind.

The women travel up to eight hours to reach the distribution point; then they wait another five hours under a blazing sun, without shade or water, to receive an insecticide-treated net for their children.

MORO MIRIRY is a nurse at the clinic hospital in Moramanga, Madagascar.

As an African woman, mother, physician, and former minister of health for the nation of Senegal, I have personally confronted the tragedy of malaria all of my life and have experienced the disease from many perspectives. As a child, I watched my siblings fall prey to it. As a young mother, I feared for the survival of my own newborn children. And as a physician, I have held other people's children in my arms, watching them die from a disease that is preventable, treatable and controllable. As minister of health, I had to make hard choices with limited resources, and like many, many others, I fought to make malaria a priority. I desperately want to see an end to this disease in my lifetime. What matters, in this case, is that the world joins together to make this possible.

MOTHERS LINE UP
in a Malagasy village to
receive measles shots and
insecticide-treated nets
for their children during
Madagascar's Mother
and Child Health Week.

ERNEST OLUOCH demon-
strates an insecticide-treated
Olyset mosquito net to
his school in Gongo village,
one of the UN Millennium
Villages in Kenya.

HUNDREDS OF THOUSANDS line up in small villages across Madagascar to receive measles shots and mosquito nets during Mother and Child Health Week.

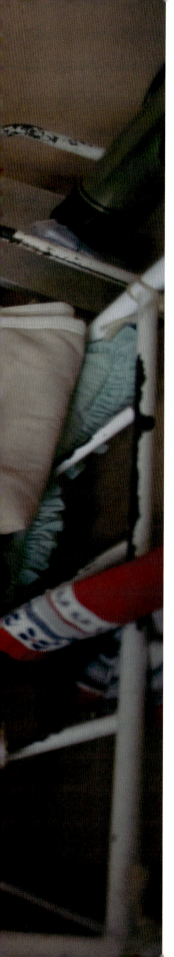

MAGGIE HALLAHAN

Maggie Hallahan (US) is a widely respected editorial and advertising photographer. Her award-winning work has been published in newspapers and magazines worldwide. After a decade as a freelance foreign correspondent based in San Francisco and Tokyo, she worked for the German magazine *Focus* as a global correspondent. Her exhibit *State of Emergency* toured California. For the past two decades Hallahan has worked for nonprofits and foundations, including the Acumen Fund, Amnesty International, the American Red Cross, Planned Parenthood, the Craigslist Foundation, the Pew Foundation, Malaria No More, Olyset Nets and the United Nations. She uses her expertise to help organizations tell their stories.

AWA MARIE COLL-SECK, MD

Awa Marie Coll-Seck, MD (Senegal), is executive director of the Roll Back Malaria Partnership, a global alliance founded in 1998 by the World Health Organization, the United Nations Development Program, the United Nations Children's Fund (UNICEF) and the World Bank with the goal of halving the world's malaria burden by 2010. Dr. Coll-Seck was formerly Senegal's minister of health and prevention, and director of policy, strategy and research for the Joint UN Program on HIV/AIDS. She is the author of more than 150 scientific publications and communications on major diseases, and has been awarded numerous professional and academic honors, including the Chevalier de l'Ordre du Mérite de la République Française, Chevalier des Palmes Académiques Françaises, Officier de l'Ordre du Mérite Sénégalais and Chevalier de l'Ordre du Mérite du Burkina Faso.

RAVELOSA BIEN AIUI FOERT in Madagascar with her one-year-old son, Mantainaiua, the first of her three children to have contracted malaria.

WHAT ONE PERSON CAN DO

The Amazing Life of Abdul Sattar Edhi

PHILANTHROPIST

Abdul Sattar Edhi with a few of the many thousands of children he has helped.

IN THE COOL INTERIOR OF A KARACHI MENTAL WARD, a short, powerfully built man with a flowing snow-white beard and dark, penetrating eyes stands beside the bed of a distraught young woman. She has covered her head with a sheet, and she cries as she pleads for news of the two children her husband took from her.

"I know you are suffering terribly, but this is no way to bring back your children," says the old man. "You have a college degree. You can do many things to help the other patients here."

"Self-help," says the old man as he walks away from the young mother's bedside. "That's the best way to get back on your feet."

For more than half a century, Abdul Sattar Edhi, now eighty years old, has proved that one determined individual can mobilize thousands of volunteers to alleviate human misery and knit together the social fabric of an entire nation. Steadfastly refusing any financial support from the Pakistani government or any organized

by **RICHARD COVINGTON**
photographs by **SHAHIDUL ALAM**

religion, this self-effacing man with a primary-school education has single-handedly created one of the largest, most successful health and welfare networks in Asia. His Edhi Foundation shelters and counsels battered wives, rescues accident victims, feeds poor children, houses homeless families, cares for the mentally incompetent, and buries unclaimed corpses. In these and many other ways, Abdul Sattar Edhi and his wife of forty-two years, Bilquis, along with a small paid staff of teachers, doctors, and nurses and more than 7,000 volunteers, help tens of thousands of Pakistanis every day.

Beginning in 1951 with a tiny 100-square-foot dispensary in Karachi's destitute Mithadar neighborhood, Edhi has struggled tirelessly to build a nationwide organization of ambulances, clinics, maternity homes, mental asylums, homes for the physically handicapped, blood banks, orphanages, adoption centers, mortuaries, shelters for runaway children and battered women, schools, nursing courses, soup kitchens—even a twenty-five-bed cancer hospital. Edhi's 600 ambulances, two airplanes, and one helicopter have saved lives in floods, earthquakes, train wrecks, civil conflicts and traffic accidents. His foundation has delivered medicines, food and clothing to refugees in Bosnia, Ethiopia and Afghanistan and continues to aid victims of the devastating October 2005 earthquake in northern Pakistan. After the 9/11 attack on the World Trade Center, Edhi donated $100,000 to Pakistanis in New York who lost their jobs as a result.

Remarkably, the lion's share of the Edhi Foundation's $10 million annual budget comes from small private donations from individuals in Pakistan and Pakistanis around the world. Edhi wants it that way. In the 1980s, when Pakistan's then-president Zia ul-Haq sent him a check for 500,000 rupees (then more than $30,000), Edhi sent it back. In 2003, the Italian government offered him a million-dollar donation, which he refused. "Governments set conditions that I cannot accept," he says, declining to elaborate.

When I visit Abdul Sattar Edhi in the bustling dispensary where he launched his vast charitable enterprise more than five decades ago, he is dressed in a simple homespun tunic over gray pajamas, scuffed sandals, and his trademark astrakhan hat. He explains his fund-raising philosophy concisely: "I tell people that, because I am working for you, the money must come from you." Indeed, for many years, Edhi personally took to the streets to beg on behalf of his growing social programs; and even now, the octogenarian activist still occasionally begs on behalf of severely ill individuals who urgently need expensive medical care that his clinics cannot provide.

Generally, however, people personally bring their small donations to one of the 300 Edhi centers and clinics across Pakistan. One such donor, who declined to give his name, explained to me that he gives money regularly to the foundation because an Edhi ambulance once rescued his sister from an automobile accident. "When I give this 1,400 rupees (US$23) to Edhi, I know it goes to people who need it," he says.

A few donors have been generous on a large scale. One family donated two villas in the wealthy Karachi suburb of Clifton, now used as a boarding school for 250 poor girls. A Pakistani expatriate in the UK donated office buildings worth more than $2.5 million that now serve as the Edhi Foundation's British headquarters. Others donate clothes, appliances, furniture—even goat and chicken meat, sometimes by the ton.

Hemmed in by a labyrinth of fabric shops, food markets, and dusty, cart-filled lanes, Edhi's three-story Mithadar center is a hive of activity, a constantly shifting scene captured indelibly by Shahidul Alam's camera on these pages. In the crowded front offices, men and women sit behind donated desks taking ambulance calls, ordering medicines, and checking the accounts of clinics and centers across the country. In another room, three women fill out adoption papers. Outside every Edhi center there is a cradle—shaded from the sun—where unwanted babies can be left anonymously. Bilquis Edhi, who oversees adoptions, has placed more than 16,000 orphans in new families.

Upstairs, a dozen infants and well-fed toddlers, some rattling across the floor in walking strollers, play and doze as Bilquis chats with a woman who has come to adopt a child for her son and daughter-in-law in the United States. "The baby she's adopting was starving when she arrived," Bilquis remarks. "When you nurse a child back to life, it really hurts to see her go, even after you've

Edhi's organization shelters and counsels battered wives, rescues accident victims, feeds poor children, houses homeless families, cares for the mentally incompetent and buries unclaimed corpses.

Taking care of my mother made me ponder the misery of others who suffered; from that time on, I began to think of how I could help them, and to dream of building hospitals and a village for the handicapped.

Top:
THE WALL of canes, crutches and walkers at Edhi Village.

Bottom:
A DISABLED CHILD at Edhi Village.

gone through the process thousands of times. But finding her a loving home makes it worth the feeling of loss."

Bilquis tells me the story of a thirty-two-year-old woman who showed up at the Mithadar clinic one day, looking for her. The woman explained that her parents had just told her that they had adopted her as an infant from the Edhi center. "I'm a doctor now, with four children of my own," she told Bilquis. "And I wanted to show my gratitude to the woman who nursed me."

"We both broke down in tears," Bilquis recalls.

With her head loosely covered by a brightly patterned yellow scarf and eyes that twinkle behind black-framed glasses, Bilquis has a sunny, lighthearted disposition that seems at odds with her husband's severe, impatient manner. They met at the clinic when she arrived as an eighteen-year-old nurse in 1965. A year or so later, they were married. Their wedding night set the tone for the relationship. Visiting his dispensary after the ceremony, Edhi found a twelve-year-old girl with severe head injuries. The newlyweds rushed her to the hospital and spent the night supervising blood transfusions and calming distraught relatives. "I didn't mind at all," Bilquis reflects. "Today that girl is married with children. That's what is really important."

Even so, Bilquis acknowledges in a playful way that life with Edhi can be trying. "Sometimes I wonder how I stayed my whole adulthood with this man who is a mental case," she says with a smile. "He won't even attend the weddings of his own children (they have four), but if there's an emergency somewhere, he'll dash out to help in an instant."

Edhi's passion for healing dates back to his childhood. At eleven, he was obliged to care for his mother, who was paralyzed with severe diabetes. "I bathed her, changed her, and fed her," he recalls in his 1996 autobiography, *A Mirror to the Blind*. "Taking care of my mother made me ponder the misery of others who suffered; from that time on, I began to think of how I could help them, and to dream of building hospitals and a village for the handicapped."

Born in 1928 in the small Indian town of Bantva in Gujarat, north of Mumbai, Edhi was "not what I would call an obedient child," he admits with a grin. Although his father made a good living brokering textiles, Edhi's parents emphasized the importance

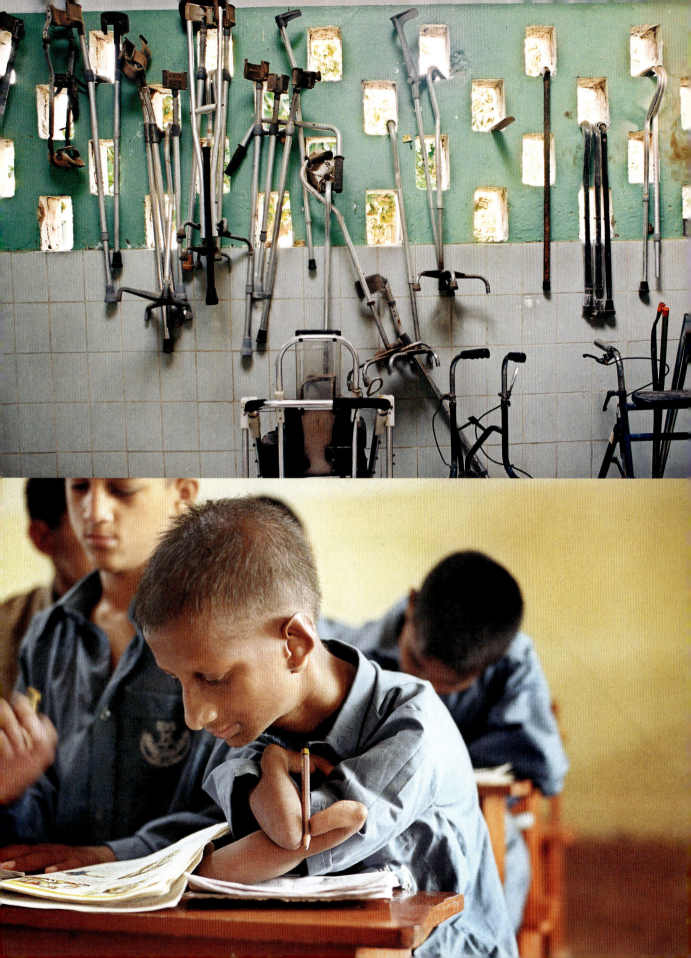

ABDUL SATTAR EDHI
in his office. He says his "computer" consists of a wall of boxes and cabinets filled with file cards.

of simplicity and frugal living. "Every day before school, my mother would give me two *paisa* and say, 'Spend one *paisa* on yourself and give the other away.' When I came home, she would ask me where I had given away my one *paisa*. It was her way of creating an awareness in me of the need for social welfare." Even now, Edhi takes no salary, instead living frugally on the interest from government bonds he bought with his inheritance and savings decades ago. The family moved from India to Karachi when the subcontinent split into the Hindu state of India and the Muslim state of Pakistan in 1947. Four years later, twenty-three-year-old Edhi used some of his savings to buy a run-down storefront. Together with a doctor who taught him the basics of health care, he set up a free dispensary. Later, he persuaded several friends to help him teach free literacy classes. At night, he slept on a cement bench outside the dispensary.

In 1957, a virulent flu epidemic swept through Karachi. Edhi used his own money to erect tented camps on the city's outskirts where people received free immunizations. When the epidemic was contained, grateful residents chipped in to expand Edhi's dispensary, enabling him to create a free maternity center and nursing school.

Soon, Edhi realized that Karachi desperately needed an ambulance service. Impressed by his efforts during the flu crisis, a local businessman donated enough money to buy a beat-up van that Edhi converted into a free ambulance that he drove himself. "I prided myself on being the first to arrive at an accident," he recalls. Today there are more than 600 Edhi ambulances nationwide, and they are credited with cutting Pakistan's annual highway fatality toll in half.

Over the years, Edhi's exploits during times of disaster have become the stuff of legend. In 1986, during a hijacking attempt, he marshaled fifty-four Edhi ambulances at Karachi airport. When Pakistani commandos stormed the plane, Edhi and his paramedics braved gunfire to save wounded passengers and crew. In 1993, during devastating floods in the Punjab, Edhi ambulances and airplanes rescued 50,000 people.

Shortly after the 2001 war in Afghanistan, Edhi set up emergency clinics on the Pakistan side of the border to treat victims. Sitting beneath anti-drug posters in the Mithadar office, Edhi's thirty-year-old son, Faisal, who also works for the foundation, vividly recalls an incident at one of these clinics, in Jamun. Local staff had purchased a dozen chairs for visiting guests and journalists. When Edhi arrived and saw the chairs, he blew up. "Why did you waste money on chairs?" he stormed. "Next you'll be buying beds for yourselves instead of spending the money on the people we intend to help." That night, to make the point, Edhi slept with the ambulance drivers on the floor of the center.

THE CALL CENTER and control room for Edhi's nationwide ambulance service.

As Faisal finishes his anecdote, Edhi rubs a hand across his balding head and nods in agreement. "People respect me because they see how simply we live and that all the donations go to the people who need help." In fact, Edhi and Bilquis, who are among Pakistan's best-known, best-respected citizens, still occupy a cramped two-room apartment next to his office inside the noisy Mithadar clinic. Edhi is on call twenty-four hours a day—just as he has been for the past fifty-six years. "I am always available to all, rich or poor," he says. "Anyone can come into this office and talk to me."

Early the next morning, I set out in an ambulance with Edhi, Faisal and longtime foundation advisor Anwer Kazmi to conduct a surprise inspection of Edhi Village. The village includes a home for runaway and abandoned boys as well as a separate asylum for mentally ill and physically handicapped men. It is a 45-minute drive south of Karachi.

At the entrance to Edhi Village, the driveway is lined with tamarisk trees covered with yellow blossoms, eucalyptus and palm trees, and beds of purple and white flowers. The courtyard is sprawling and grassy, surrounded by classrooms and dormitories. It contains a playground, a soccer field, and volleyball and basketball courts. "Faisal organized the boys to do the landscaping," Edhi says proudly. "It's part of our self-help initiative."

When Edhi purchased the village's 26-hectare (65-acre) parcel in 1985, it was barren land. Now there are kitchens, workshops, recreation rooms, and housing for 250 children in one complex and 1,500 mental patients in another. In one of the classrooms, Edhi singles out an alert ten-year-old pupil with a congenitally deformed hand. "When he was a newborn, this boy was abandoned in one of our cradles outside a center in Karachi," Edhi tells me. "Bilquis named him Shazab and took care of him in Mithadar until he was old enough to come here. Now he's one of our smartest students." When Edhi asks him what he'd like to do when he graduates, Shazab breaks into a shy smile. "I want to be in charge of Edhi Village," he says.

Back in Karachi, Edhi expertly maneuvers the ambulance through teeming streets to his women's sanatorium in north Karachi. As he ambles down the immaculate marble hallways, residents cluster around him, calling *"Abu-ji!"* ("Honored Daddy!")

Previous pages:
AN EDHI AMBULANCE parked in front of the Edhi Information Bureau and the Edhi Free Kitchen in Karachi, Pakistan. Ambulances were the first service provided by the Edhi Foundation in the 1950s.

Following pages, clockwise from top left:
NURSES FEED a tuberculosis patient at an Edhi hospital; a computer class at the Edhi Training Center at the Clifton Home in Karachi; the cancer ward at the Edhi Foundation Hospital in Karachi; the playground at Edhi Village.

"This adulation makes me nervous," he confides to me. "I'm not some kind of saint."

One woman sits on concrete steps, distractedly waving flies away from an open sore on her foot. Edhi bends close, asking her gently how long it has been infected. "Two days," she replies, "but it's much worse this afternoon." He shouts for a nurse. When no one comes, he stalks away impatiently. "Don't worry," he calls over his shoulder. "I'll be back with a bandage before you know it."

After Edhi has disinfected and dressed the woman's wound, he sits on a stone bench and listens as one resident after another tells him heartrending stories of cruel husbands and family betrayal. Driving back to the Mithadar center, he vents his long-running frustrations about the plight of women in Pakistan. "Society here goes against the teachings of the Qur'an in mistreating women and not giving them equality," he says with indignation. "Only 10 percent of Pakistani women know how to read and write. That's why we try so hard to give the girls who come to us a good education. Once they get an education, they can take control of their lives."

Back at Mithadar, a businessman in a crisp linen shirt and polished shoes waits for Edhi in his office. "Here's one who has come around," he says, gripping the man's shoulders in a friendly embrace. Edhi explains that the businessman has launched a partnership with the foundation to help poor men and women start fabric shops, food stalls and other small businesses.

"He's helping them stand on their own rather than giving them handouts that only make them more dependent," says Abdul Sattar Edhi with a weary smile. "That's the humanitarian revolution we need. But still so few understand. Let's spread the word."

Not everyone can be a philanthropic visionary like Edhi, and few would want to be as single-minded and demanding, the so-called mental case that his own wife tolerates. But Edhi's drive for action, not simply talk, is humbling. His brand of charity lies at the heart of the most fundamental Muslim—and Christian, Jewish, Hindu, Buddhist and Sikh—beliefs and imperatives, and it is a shining, insistent testimony that one person can make a difference and better the lives of millions.

People respect us because they see how simply we live and that all the donations go to the people who need help.

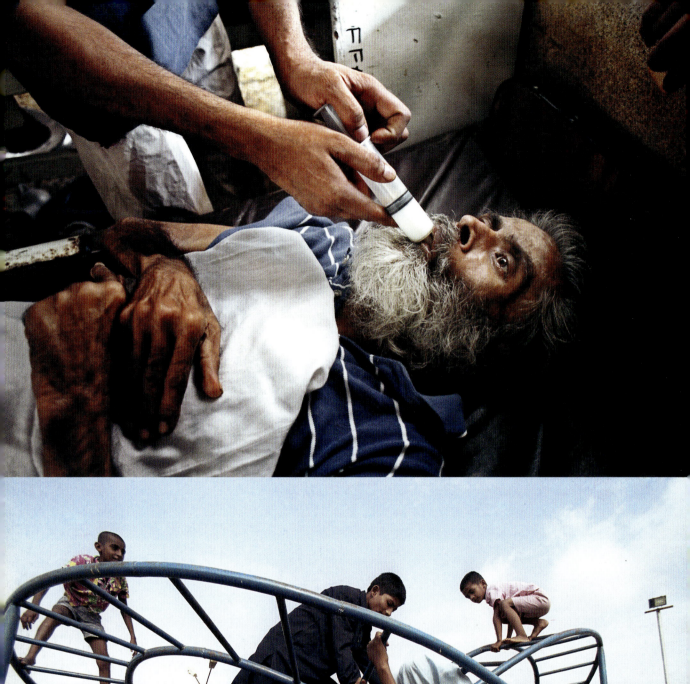

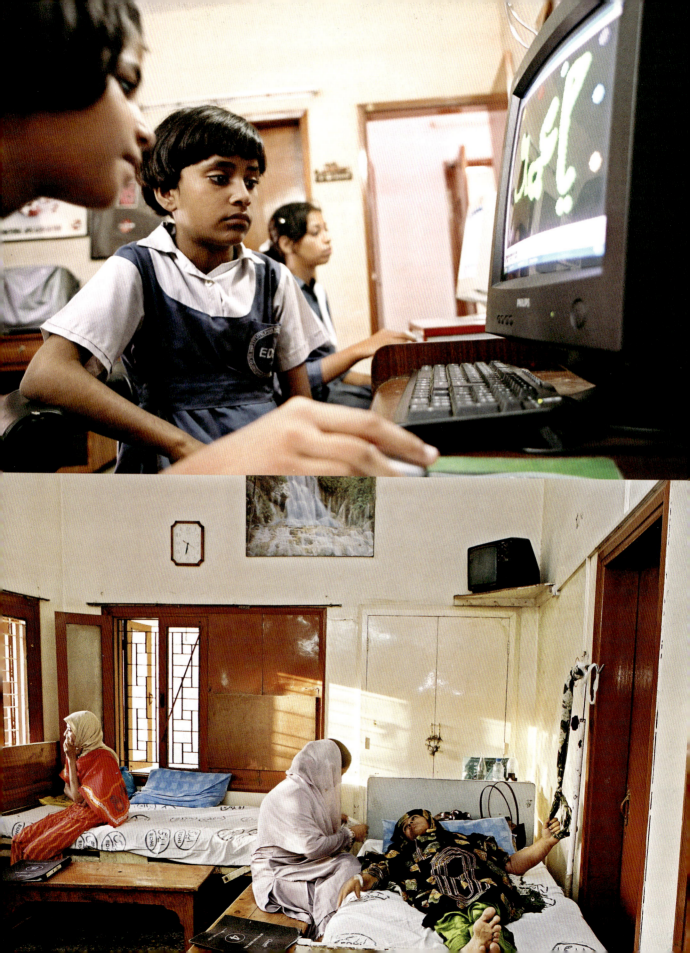

SHAHIDUL ALAM

Photojournalist and critic Shahidul Alam (Bangladesh) is the founder of Drik, Bangladesh's first photography library and gallery, as well as Pathshala, the South Asian Institute of Photography. Alam's work has been published in many international publications, including *Time, Newsweek, The New York Times* and *The Guardian*, and has been exhibited in prestigious venues worldwide, including New York's Museum of Modern Art, the Pompidou Center in Paris, the Museum of Contemporary Arts in Tehran and the Photographer's Gallery in London.

RICHARD COVINGTON

Paris-based author Richard Covington (US) has traveled with nomads in Saudi Arabia, picked tomatoes with migrant workers in South Florida, tracked copyright piracy in China and Hong Kong, investigated unsafe nuclear power plants in Eastern Europe and depicted post-conflict Beirut, Bosnia and Rwanda. He has written about art, archaeology and heritage in Morocco, Egypt, Iran, Afghanistan, Burma, Cambodia and Europe. Covering a wide range of cultural and historical subjects, he has contributed to *Smithsonian, The New York Times, The International Herald Tribune, The Los Angeles Times, The Sunday Times of London, Reader's Digest, Art in America* and Salon.com. A fan of French history, he has published biographical profiles of Napoleon, Charlemagne and Marie Antoinette. His most recent project details the cultural transformation of the Silk Road, reporting from Kazakhstan and Uzbekistan to Istanbul and Venice.

ABDUL SATTAR EDHI and his wife and partner, Bilquis Edhi, share a simple breakfast at their original Mithadar clinic. As much as any two people, they epitomize the wonderful possibilities of individual initiative.

WHAT YOU CAN DO

193 Ways
to Learn More and
Get Involved

MELTDOWN

Save energy in your home and car:

www.aceee.org/Consumer/index.htm
American Council for an Energy Efficient Economy

Find energy-efficient appliances for your home and business:

www.energystar.gov
Energy Star (The US Environmental Protection Agency
    and US Department of Energy)

Reduce your environmental impact:

www.climate.org
Climate Institute

Help your business become more environmentally responsible:

www.climatebiz.com
Greener World Media Network

Find lesson plans about climate change:

How We Know What We Know About Our
    Changing Climate: Scientists and Kids Explore
    Global Warming, Lynne Cherry and Gary Braasch,
    Dawn Publications, 2008

www.climatechangeeducation.org
Climate Change Education, University of California,
    Berkeley

Donate to organizations working to reduce global warming:

ww2.earthday.net/~earthday/
Earth Day Network

www.nrdc.org
Natural Resources Defense Council

Learn more about the science of climate change:

www.climatechallenge.gov.uk/
Climate Change Communication Initiative (led by Defra,
    a department of the British government)

www.ucsusa.org/global_warming/science/
Union of Concerned Scientists

www.un.org/climatechange/index.shtml
UN Climate Change Activities

See more of Gary Braasch's photographs of climate change:

www.worldviewofglobalwarming.org
The Blue Earth Alliance

Earth Under Fire: How Global Warming is Changing
    the World, Gary Braasch, University of California
    Press, 2007
www.earthunderfire.com

Read more of Bill McKibben's thoughts about climate change and join his call to action:

www.billmckibben.com

The End of Nature, Bill McKibben, Random House
    Trade Paperbacks, 2006

Fight Global Warming Now: The Handbook for Taking
    Action in Your Community, Bill McKibben, Holt, 2007

ECONOMIC MIRACLE, ENVIRONMENTAL DISASTER

Learn more about pollution in China:

www.nrdc.org/air/energy/china/default.asp
The Natural Resources Defense Council

Donate to organizations working to reduce pollution in China:

www.greengrants.org/index.php
Global Greengrants Fund

www.greenpeace.org/china/en/
Greenpeace China

www.panda.org/how_you_can_help/
World Wildlife Fund

See more of Stephen Voss's photographs of the Huai River Basin:

www.stephenvoss.com/stories/ChinaWaterPollution/

Read more of Elizabeth C. Economy's thoughts on pollution in China:

The River Runs Black: The Environmental Challenge to China's Future, Elizabeth C. Economy, Cornell University Press, 2004

"China vs. Earth," Elizabeth C. Economy, *The Nation*, May 7, 2007
www.thenation.com/doc/20070507/economy

"Scorched Earth," Elizabeth C. Economy, *Harvard Business Review*, June 2007
http://harvardbusinessonline.hbsp.harvard.edu/hbsp/hbr/articles/article.jsp?articleID=R0706F&ml_action=get-article&print=true

"The Great Leap Backward?" Elizabeth C. Economy, *Foreign Affairs*, September/October 2007
www.foreignaffairs.org/20070901faessay86503/elizabeth-c-economy/the-great-leap-backward.html

THIRSTY WORLD

Donate to organizations working to provide clean water:

www.africare.org/
Africare

www.globalwater.org/help.htm
Global Water

www.wateraid.org/international/donate/
Water Aid

www.water.org/waterpartners.aspx?pgID=923
Water Partners International

Get information on water-related topics, including pictures, maps and data:

www.circleofblue.org
Circle of Blue (an affiliate of the Pacific Institute)

Get lesson plans about safe water, sanitation and sustainable water resources:

www.wateraid.org/international/learn_zone/
Water Aid

http://ga.water.usgs.gov/edu/
United States Geological Survey

See more of Brent Stirton's photographs of the water crisis in developing countries:

www.brentstirton.com/feature-water_issues.php

Read more of Peter H. Gleick's thoughts on the water crisis in developing countries:

www.worldwater.org
The World's Water (a project of the Pacific Institute)

www.pacinst.org/
Pacific Institute

The World's Water: The Biennial Report on Freshwater Resources, Peter H. Gleick, Gary H. Wolff and Heather Cooley, Island Press, 2006
www.islandpress.org/books/detail.html/SKU/1-59726-106-8

FALLOUT

Donate to an organization working for Chernobyl victims:

www.chernobyl-international.com/sponsor/sponsor.544.html
Chernobyl Children's Project International

Learn more about the Chernobyl disaster:

The Social Impact of the Chernobyl Disaster, David R. Marples, St. Martin's Press, 1988

Nuclear Energy and Security in the Former Soviet Union, David R. Marples and Marilyn J. Young, editors, Perseus, 1997

Voices from Chernobyl: The Oral History of a Nuclear Disaster, Svetlana Alexievich, Picador, 2006

Chernobyl Legacy, Paul Fusco, photographer, de.MO, 2001

Zones of Exclusion: Pripyat and Chernobyl, Robert Polidori, photographer, Steidl/Pace/MacGill Gallery, 2003

Learn more about children born with heart defects after Chernobyl:

Chernobyl Heart, directed by Maryann De Leo, HBO Documentary Films, 2003
www.hbo.com/docs/programs/chernobylheart/

See more of Gerd Ludwig's photographs of Chernobyl:

www.gerdludwig.com

www7.nationalgeographic.com/ngm/0604/sights_n_sounds/
National Geographic

IMAGES OF GENOCIDE

Join the anti-genocide movement:

www.genocideintervention.net/user/register
Genocide Intervention Network

Donate to organizations protecting genocide victims:

www.icrc.org
International Committee of the Red Cross (ICRC)

www.aegistrust.org
Aegis (UK)

www.hrw.org/
Human Rights Watch

For more information on genocide:

www.ushmm.org/conscience/alert/darfur/what/en/
United States Holocaust Memorial Museum

www.threegenerations.org/Take_Action/take_action.html
Three Generations

Hotel Rwanda, directed by Terry George,
    Lion's Gate Films/United Artists, 2004

See more photographs by Magnum photographers:

www.magnumphotos.com

*Magnum: Fifty Years at the Front Line of History:
    The Story of the Legendary Photo Agency*, Russell
    Miller, Grove Press, 1999

Magnum Magnum, Brigitte Lardinois,
    Thames & Hudson, November 30, 2007

Read more of Omer Bartov's thoughts on genocide:

www.brown.edu/Departments/History/people/faculty
    page.php?id=1106970215

*In God's Name: Genocide and Religion in the Twentieth
    Century*, Omer Bartov and Phyllis Mack, Berghahn
    Books, 2001

*Mirrors of Destruction: War, Genocide, and Modern
    Identity*, Omer Bartov, Oxford University Press, 2000

Crimes of War: Guilt and Denial in the Twentieth Century,
    Omer Bartov, Atina Grossmann and Mary Noland, The
    New Press, 2002

Germany's War and the Holocaust: Disputed Histories,
    Omer Bartov, Cornell University Press, 2003

*Murder in Our Midst: The Holocaust, Industrial Killing,
    and Representation*, Omer Bartov, Oxford
    University Press, 1996

THE SCORCHED EARTH OF DARFUR

Learn more about the Darfur conflict:

www.eyesondarfur.org/crisis.html
Eyes on Darfur (a project of Amnesty International, in
    partnership with the Crisis Prevention and Response
    Center and the Save Darfur Coalition)

www.enoughproject.org/
A project of the International Crisis Group and the Center
    for American Progress

See satellite images showing the destruction in Darfur:

www.eyesondarfur.org/satellite.html
Eyes on Darfur

Donate to organizations working to end the genocide in Darfur, or volunteer your time:

www.helpdarfurnow.org/donate.php
Help Darfur Now
www.dpado.org/help.php
Darfur Peace and Development Organization

www.darfurrehab.org/volunteer.htm
Darfur Rehabilitation Project

Encourage divestment from companies doing business with Sudan:

www.sudandivestment.org/getInvolved.asp
Genocide Intervention Network

Donate to an organization helping Darfur refugees obtain political asylum:

www.damanga.org/donations/index.html
Damanga Coalition for Freedom and Democracy

Learn more about the United Nations' role in the Darfur conflict:

"On Our Watch," *Frontline*, directed by Neil Docherty, 2007
www.pbs.org/wgbh/pages/frontline/darfur/

The Devil Came on Horseback, directed by Annie
    Sundberg and Ricki Stern, in partnership with Global
    Grassroots, 2007

See your US legislator's record on Darfur:

www.darfurscores.org/
Genocide Intervention Network

See more photographs by Marcus Bleasdale:

www.marcusbleasdale.com/

Read more of Samantha Power's thoughts on genocide:

"A Problem from Hell": America and the Age of Genocide,
    Samantha Power, Basic Books, 2002

Read more of John Prendergast's thoughts on Darfur:

*Not on Our Watch: A Mission to End Genocide in Darfur
    and Beyond*, Don Cheadle and John Prendergast,
    Hyperion, 2007
www.notonourwatchbook.com/

GLOBAL JIHAD

Read more of Fawaz A. Gerges' thoughts on the global jihad:

Journey of the Jihadist: Inside Muslim Militancy,
    Fawaz A. Gerges, Harcourt, 2007

The Far Enemy: Why Jihad Went Global, Fawaz A. Gerges,
    Cambridge University Press, 2005

BITTER FRUIT

Donate to organizations providing emergency assistance to the families of US soldiers serving, injured or killed in the Iraq war:

www.operationhomefront.net/donate.htm
Operation Home Front

www.fallenpatriotfund.org
Fallen Patriot Fund

www.fisherhouse.org/contribute/onlineGiving.shtml
Fisher House (in partnership with Caring Bridge)

www.taps.org/contributions/donate.aspx
Tragedy Assistance Program for Survivors

Purchase a certificate of deposit that supports family members of US veterans:

www.veteransfamilyfund.org/wheretobuy
Veterans Family Fund

Donate to an organization working to rehabilitate wounded servicemen and women:

www.operationsecondchance.org/Donate.htm
Operation Second Chance

Donate to an organization of military widows and widowers whose spouses died on active duty or from service-connected disabilities:

www.goldstarwives.org
Gold Star Wives of America

See more of Paul Fusco's photographs of Iraqi war victims' funerals:

www.magnumphotos.com
Magnum Photos

Read more of Gary Kamiya's thoughts on the Iraq war:

"Breaking the Iraq Stalemate," Gary Kamiya, Salon.com,
    September 18, 2007
www.salon.com/opinion/kamiya/2007/09/18/iraq_stalemate/

THE BOTTOM BILLION

Donate to organizations working to combat global poverty:

www.pih.org/youcando/donate.html
Partners in Health

www.bridgestoprosperity.org/donors.htm
Bridges to Prosperity

www.ewb-usa.org/donate.php
Engineers without Borders

Become a member of the global anti-poverty movement:

www.one.org/about/
The One Campaign

Donate to organizations working to end global hunger:

www.wfp.org
United Nations World Food Program

www.actionagainsthunger.org/
Action Against Hunger

Make microloans to entrepreneurs and small businesses in the developing world:

www.namaste-direct.org/
NamasteDirect

www.kiva.org/about/how/
Kiva

Get a list of anti-poverty campaigns in the UK:

www.makepovertyhistory.org/keepcampaigning/
Make Poverty History

See more photographs by James Nachtwey:

www.jamesnachtwey.com

Read more of Jeffrey D. Sachs' thoughts on ending poverty:

www.unmillenniumproject.org
UN Millennium Project

The End of Poverty: Economic Possibilities for Our Time,
    Jeffrey D. Sachs, Penguin, 2006

SHOP 'TIL WE DROP

Learn more about fighting rampant consumerism:

www.newdream.org/tttoffline/actions.php
New American Dream

www.storyofstuff.com
The Story of Stuff

www.commercialalert.org/
Commercial Alert

Get lesson plans about consumerism and its effects:

www.pbs.org/kcts/affluenza/treat/tguide/tguide.html
PBS: *Affluenza*

Learn more about simpler, sustainable living:

http://lighterfootstep.com/2.html
Lighter Footstep

www.eartheasy.com/homepage.htm
Eartheasy

www.thegreenguide.com/
National Geographic Green Guide

Get a guide to responsible purchasing:

www.responsiblepurchasing.org/purchasing_guides/all/
Responsible Purchasing Network

See more of Lauren Greenfield's work:

www.laurengreenfield.com/

Thin, Lauren Greenfield, Chronicle Books, 2006

Thin, directed by Lauren Greenfield,
    HBO Documentary Films, 2006
Available on DVD at http://store.HBO.com

Fast Forward: Growing Up in the Shadow of Hollywood,
Lauren Greenfield, Chronicle Books, 2004

Girl Culture, Lauren Greenfield, Chronicle Books, 2002
www.girlculture.com

kids + money, directed by Lauren Greenfield, HBO
    Documentary Films, 2008
www.kidsandmoney.tv

**Read more of Juliet B. Schor's thoughts
on consumerism:**

*The Overspent American: Why We Want What We
    Don't Need*, Juliet Schor, HarperCollins, 2006

*Born to Buy: The Commercialized Child and the
    Consumer Culture*, Juliet Schor, Scribner, 2005

Or watch:

*The Overspent American: Why We Want What We
    Don't Need*, produced by Loretta Alper and
    Sut Jhally, The Media Education Foundation, 2004

CHILDREN OF THE BLACK DUST

Donate to organizations protecting children's rights:

www.supportunicef.org
UNICEF

www.hrw.org/act/act.html
Human Rights Watch

www.incidinb.org/index1024.htm
Incidin Bangladesh

www.afop.org/childlabor.htm
Association of Farm Worker Opportunity Programs

Get a lesson plan about child labor in America:

www.memory.loc.gov/learn/lessons/98/labor/plan.html
The Library of Congress

**Learn more about child welfare
in specific countries:**

www.unicef.org/infobycountry/
UNICEF

See more of Shehzad Noorani's photographs:

www.fiftycrows.org/photoessay/noorani/index.php
FiftyCrows: Social Change Photography

www.unicef.org/photoessays/41908.html
UNICEF

www.globalizingworld.net/noorani.html
Tales from a Globalizing World

LOST GIRLS

**Donate to organizations working to help
child brides and women globally:**

www.icrw.org/html/donate/donate_ask.htm
International Center for Research on Women

www.popcouncil.org/supporting/AdolGirlsContribute.html
Population Council

www.medicamondiale.org/_en/
Medica Mondiale

**Learn more about current child bride-related
legislation:**

www.iwhc.org/getinvolved
International Women's Health Coalition

Take action against child marriage:

www.pbs.org/now/shows/341/take-action.html
PBS: "Child Brides," NOW

www.womenforwomen.org/mkdiff.htm
Women for Women International

**Donate to organizations providing aid
to girls and women globally:**

www.equalitynow.org
Equality Now

www.etwla.org/index.htm
Ethiopian Women Lawyers Association

**Donate to an organization working
to stop the trafficking of women:**

www.catwinternational.org/
Coalition Against Trafficking in Women

See more of Stephanie Sinclair's photographs:

www.stephaniesinclair.com

**Read more of Judith Bruce's thoughts on
child marriage:**

"The Diverse Universe of Adolescents, and the Girls and
    Boys Left Behind," Judith Bruce and Erica Chong, UN
    Millennium Project, 2006
www.unmillenniumproject.org/documents/Bruce_
    and_Chong-final.pdf

"Protecting Young Women from HIV/AIDS:
    The Case Against Child and Adolescent Marriage,"
    Shelley Clark, Judith Bruce and Annie Dude,
    International Family Planning Perspectives, June 2006
www.guttmacher.org/pubs/journals/3207906.pdf

"Child Marriage in the Context of the HIV Epidemic,"
    Judith Bruce, Population Council, September 2007
www.popcouncil.org/pdfs/TABriefs/PGY_Brief11_
    ChildMarriageHIV.pdf

Or watch:

"Child Brides: Stolen Lives," NOW, produced by
    Amy Bucher, 2007
www.pbs.org/now/shows/341/index.html

THE PRICE OF OUR OIL ADDICTION

Learn more about the social and environmental issues in the Niger Delta:

www.eraction.org/
Environmental Rights Action (Nigerian chapter of Friends of the Earth International)

www.icg.org
International Crisis Group

www.hrw.org/doc/?t=africa&c=niger
Human Rights Watch

www.waado.org/Environment/EnvironmentPage.html
Urhobo Historical Society

Learn more about corporate accountability in the oil industry:

www.stopcorporateabuse.org/cms/page1112.cfm
Corporate Accountability International

www.corpwatch.org
CorpWatch

www.platformlondon.org/carbonweb/
Unraveling the Carbon Web (a project by Platform)

Learn more about alternatives to oil:

http://gx.freedomfromoil.org/alternatives/
Global Exchange

http://ran.freedomfromoil.org/
Rainforest Action Network

See more of Ed Kashi's photographs of the Niger Delta:

www.edkashi.com/

Curse of the Black Gold, Ed Kashi and Michael Watts, Powerhouse Books, 2008

To read more of Michael Watts' thoughts on the Niger Delta:

http://geography.berkeley.edu/PeopleHistory/faculty/
    M_Watts.html

http://geography.berkeley.edu/ProjectsResources/
    ND%20Website/NigerDelta/index.html
Niger Delta Economies of Violence Project

Learn more about the politics of oil:

Untapped: The Scramble for Africa's Oil, John Ghazvinian, Harcourt, 2007

Oil Wars, Mary Kaldor, Terry L. Karl and Yahia Said, Pluto Press, 2007

The Next Gulf: London, Washington and Oil Conflict in Nigeria, Andrew Rowell, James Marriott and Lorne Stockman, 2005

Oil and Politics in the Gulf of Guinea, Ricardo Soares de Oliveira, Columbia University Press, 2007

High Stakes and Stakeholders: Oil Conflict in Nigeria, Kenneth Omeje, Ashgate, 2006

THE GREATEST MIGRATION

Learn more about global urbanization:

http://news.bbc.co.uk/2/hi/in_depth/world/2006/
    urbanisation/default.stm
BBC: Urban Planet

Donate to an organization working to improve conditions for migrants:

www.iom.int/jahia/Jahia/pid/2
International Organization for Migration

See more photographs by Sebastião Salgado:

www.terra.com.br/sebastiaosalgado/

Migrations, Sebastião Salgado, Aperture, 2005

Africa, Sebastião and Leila Salgado and Mia Couto, Taschen, 2007

Sebastião Salgado: Workers, Aperture, 2005

Read more of Paul Knox's thoughts:

Urbanization: An Introduction to Urban Geography, Paul Knox, Prentice Hall, 2005

THE FENCE

Donate to organizations working toward immigration reform:

www.ailf.org/
American Immigration Law Foundation

www.cirnow.org/content/en/donation.htm
Coalition for Comprehensive Immigration Reform

Donate to an organization working to protect immigrant rights:

www.rcusa.org/index.php?page=about-us
Refugee Council USA

Donate to organizations that protect the rights of Latino immigrants and their families:

www.nilc.org/
National Immigration Law Center

www.nclr.org/
National Council for La Raza

www.maldef.org
Mexican American Legal Defense and Education Fund

See more of Anthony Suau's photographs of the US-Mexico border:

www.archive.anthonysuau.com

See other photographs by Anthony Suau:

Fear This, Anthony Suau and Chris Hedges, Aperture, 2005

Read more of Douglas S. Massey's thoughts on immigration policy:

Beyond Smoke and Mirrors: Mexican Immigration in an Era of Economic Integration, Douglas Massey, Russell Sage Foundation Publications, 2003

Crossing the Border: Research from the Mexican Migration Project, Douglas Massey, Russell Sage Foundation Publications, August 2006

INFECTED OR AFFECTED

Donate to organizations supporting HIV and AIDS research:

www.aidsresearch.org/
AIDS Research Alliance

www.amfar.org/cgi-bin/iowa/support
American Medical Foundation for AIDS Research

Donate to organizations working to stop the spread of AIDS and HIV:

www.globalaidsalliance.org/page/contribute/
Global AIDS Alliance

www.helpchildrenwithaids.org/donate.htm
American Foundation for Children with AIDS

Get a lesson plan about the AIDS epidemic:

www.nationalgeographic.com/xpeditions/lessons/
11/g912/trade.html
National Geographic

Find local opportunities to get involved in AIDS activism:

www.aidsalliance.org/sw45117.asp?
International HIV/AIDS Alliance

See more of Tom Stoddart's photographs:

www.tomstoddart.com

iWitness, Tom Stoddart, Trolley, 2004

Read more of Helen Epstein's thoughts about the AIDS epidemic:

The Invisible Cure: Africa, the West, and the Fight Against AIDS, Helen Epstein, Farrar, Straus and Giroux, 2007

THE END OF MALARIA?

Learn more about global efforts to fight malaria:

www.rollbackmalaria.org
Rollback Malaria Partnership

www.malaria.org
Malaria Foundation International

Volunteer with an organization fighting malaria:

www.gatesfoundation.org/AboutUs/WorkingWithUs/
GettingInvolved/
Bill & Melinda Gates Foundation

Donate to organizations researching affordable antimalarial drugs:

www.mmv.org/rubrique.php3?id_rubrique=6
Medicines for Malaria Venture

www.malariavaccine.org/contribute.htm
Malaria Vaccine Initiative (a program of PATH)

Donate insecticide-treated antimalarial mosquito nets:

www.unfoundation.org/campaigns/nothing_but_nets/
donate.asp
UN Foundation

www.vetothesquito.org/donate.html
Veto the 'Squito (part of the Malaria No More Network)

Learn about other ways to take action against the spread of malaria:

www.malarianomore.org/get_involved.php
Malaria No More

Get lesson plans about malaria:

www.malarianomore.org/kids/educational-materials.php
Malaria No More

See more of Maggie Hallahan's photographs:

www.maggiehallahan.com/

WHAT ONE PERSON CAN DO

Donate to the Edhi Foundation:

www.edhi.org/donate.htm
Edhi Foundation

Or write to:

USA

45-11 National Street
Corona, NY 11368
Phone: +1 (718) 639-0633
Fax: +1 (718) 505-8001

UK

316 Edgware Road
London, England W2 1DY
Phone: +44 (207) 723-2050
Fax: +44 (207) 224-9774
E-mail: edhiuk@yahoo.com

CANADA

Canada Edhi Charitable Foundation, Inc.
257 Risebrough Circe
Markham, ON L3R 3J3

INDEX

INDEX

INDEX

INDEX

THANKS

What Matters is dedicated to my amazing children, Kara, Will, Lucas, Angela and Grace, and my beautiful wife, Laureen, whose talent, intellect, integrity, love and patience inspire me every day. —*dec*

WHAT MATTERS STAFF

Produced and directed by
David Elliot Cohen
Book design and layout by
Lori Barra
and **Margaret Swart**
Design assistant, **Sarah Kessler**
Color management and image
processing by **Peter Truskier**,
Premedia Systems, Inc.
Associate Producer, **Heather King**
"What You Can Do" section
compiled by our editorial assistant,
Rose Whitmore
Copyedited by **Sherri Schultz**
Proofread by **Sharon Vonasch**
Index by **Nanette Cardon**

THANKS, ALSO, TO

Mikkel Aaland
Acumen Fund
Tina Ahrens, *GEO* Magazine
Isabel Allende
Nicolás Frías Allende
Juliette Ambatzidis,
    The Isabel Allende Foundation
Leigh Ann Ambrosi,
    Sterling Publishing
Kelly Anderson, The Associated Press
Asociación de Médicos Vegetalistas
    de Iquitos (Peru)
Jonathan Auch,
    James Nachtwey Studio
Aveda
Ishan Banerjee,
    Sarah Lawrence College
Brooke Barona, Sterling Publishing
Frank, Thomas, James, Allison, Joseph,
    Julia and Isabel Barra
Tom and Lucille Barra
Sunny Bates, Sunny Bates Associates
Jill Benson, The Population Council
Barbara Berger, Sterling Publishing
Carole Bidnick
Jeffery Bleich,
    Munger, Tolles & Olsen
Blue Earth Alliance
Jeff Boettcher
Alexandra Botwin
Joann Boyles
The Braasch Family
Toni Brayer & Craig Patterson
Caroline Brown, Sterling Publishing
Molly Browning, Enough Project
Stephanie Bruce
Jennifer Cho, Millennium Promise
Dan and Stacy Cohen
Hannah and Norman Cohen
Nadia Cohen, VII Photos
Contact Press Images
Caroline Cortizo

Elias Courson
Lauren Cuthbert
Dr. Eric Deharo
Wendie Demuth
Alex Dewaal
Discover Magazine
Oronto Douglas
Jeff Duda
Saida Emami
Jeffrey Epstein
Andrew Erlichson, Phanfare
Frank Evers
Philip Feldman, Coblentz, Patch,
    Duffy & Bass
Fifty Crows Foundation
Janine Firpo
Vivienne Flesher
Guido and Rossana Fraeme
Michael Fragnito, Sterling Publishing
Alejandro, Andrea and Nicole Frías
Yury and Zhenya Friedman
Peter and Margot Friend
Dr. Dioni Gamboa
J. Carl Ganter, Circle of Blue
Marina Gavrioushkina
Elizabeth Gebhardt
GEO Magazine, Germany
Getty Images
Kevin Gilbert, Blue Pixel
Alexei Girard, 6Sight
Rena Golden, CNN
Lisa Goldman,
    Sumitomo Global Vector Control
Lynn Goldsmith
William C. Gordon
Dr. Mark Grabowsky
Mark Greenberg
The Guggenheim Foundation
Nicole Haberland,
    The Population Council
David Hagerman
Dylan Hallahan
Nathaniel Hang
Michael Hicks,
    James Nachtwey Studio
Dana Hilmer
Hospital Nacional Cayetano Heredia
Peter Howe
Human Rights Watch
Institut Malgache de Recherches
    Appliquées (Madagascar)
Instituto de Medicina Tropical
Instituto de Investigaciones
    de La Amazonía Peruana
International League of Conservation
    Photographers
International Wildlife Magazine
Nate James
Amanda Jones
Charlene Kannankeril
Steve and Jill Kantola
Sarah, Scott and Nora Kessler

Warren King
Douglas and Francoise Kirkland
Tad Kirschner
Amy Klostermann
Kalee Kreider, Carthage Group
Susanne Krieg
Eliane Laffont
Sangeeta Lama
Jaeah J. Lee, The Council on Foreign
    Relations
Dr. Alejandro Lianos
The Library and Archives Canada
Jodi Lipe, Current
liveBooks
Livingstone Membiere
Dolores Lusitana, Gerd Ludwig
    Photography
Magnum Photos
Malaria No More
Nadja Masri, *GEO*
Margaret McGurk
The McGurk Family
Sharon McKenna
Medecins Sans Frontieres
Douglas Menuez
David and Lisa Monetta
Regine Moylett
Diane Murray
Corinne Nagy
National Geographic Magazine
National Science Foundation
Natural Resources Defense Council
Lori Needleman,
    Lauren Greenfield Photography
New York Times Magazine
Milka Njunge
Dr. William M. Novick, International
    Children's Heart Foundation
Jacqueline Novogratz, Acumen Fund
Our Niger Delta (Nigeria)
Andy Patrick,
    Fifty Crows Foundation
The Peralta Family
E. Gabriel Perle
Liz Perle
Paola Piazza,
    Roll Back Malaria Partnership
Francois Piffard, Amazonas Images
Elias Piniela
Robert Pledge, Contact Press Images
The Population Council
Gina Privitere, *The New York Times*
Mitchell Prothero
Kathleen Pullum
Christof Putzel, Current
The Andry Ramandason Family
Dimison Ramandason
Prof. Elfie Raymond,
    Sarah Lawrence College
Prof. Eric Reeves, Smith College
Spencer Reiss, *Wired Magazine*
Dr. Elsa Rengifo

Len and Steve Riggio,
    Barnes & Noble
Denise Rocco-Zilber
Adi Roche, Chernobyl Children's
    Project International
Roll Back Malaria Partnership
Annika Rosenblatt,
    The Earth Institute
Kathy Ryan, *The New York Times*
Fawad Sahil
Leila Salgado, Amazonas Images
Mizuno San
J. Curtis Sanburn
Alexander Sanchez
Dr. Michel Sausin
Gilles Saussier
Aimee Segal
Courtney Smith, The Pacific Institute
Jeffrey D. Smith, Contact Press Images
Prudence Smith,
    Roll Back Malaria Partnership
Rick Smolan
Sarah Stanlick, Harvard University
Erick and Lisa Steinberg
Brian Storm, Media Storm
Sumitomo Global Vector Control
Ellen Tolmie, UNICEF
Denise Trabona
Unidad de Parasitología Celular
Universidad Peruana
University of California Press
VII Photos
Dimieari von Kemedi
Alexander von Perfall
Susan Wels
Wiancko Family Fund
Joanna Wieland
Tony White,
    White & Black Lab, London
Maura Whitmore
Julie Winokur, Talking Eyes Media
Lily Yekoye
Tony Zweig

AND, PARTICULARLY . . .

Huo Daishan, the humble activist,
    who has made saving the Huai
    River his life's work and has
    suffered the consequences.
Our very smart and thoroughly
    delightful literary agent,
    Carol Mann
Ajmal Naqeshbandi, who was
    killed by the Taliban, for his work
    with foreign journalists on the issue
    of Afghan child marriage.
Michael Shulman of Magnum
    Photos, who came through when
    we most needed help.